Toward Urban Economic Vibrancy

Patterns and Practices in Asia's New Cities

Edited by **SIQI ZHENG** and **ZHENGZHEN TAN**

SA+P Press
MIT School of Architecture and Planning

Designed by Louis Charron

Distributed by the MIT Press
Cambridge, Massachusetts
London, England

Content

Acknowledgments

We are grateful to external reviewers for their truly helpful comments and suggestions (in alphabetical order): Dennis Frenchman (MIT) for chapter 9; Yuming Fu (National University of Singapore) for chapter 2, 3 and 4; Richard Peiser (Harvard University) for chapter 8; Sandy Pentland (MIT) for chapter 5; Brent Ryan (MIT) for chapter 6, 7 and 9; Bish Sanyal (MIT) for chapter 1.

We would like to thank our colleagues and students in the Department of Urban Studies and Planning and the Center for Real Estate at the Massachusetts Institute of Technology for their support and intellectual inspiration. We thank Patsy Baudoin and Melissa Vaughn for their collaboration in editing the manuscript and guiding us through the book project.

We thank the MIT China Future City Research Consortium for their support of our lab's multiple research projects over the past three years, including this one. The consortium members are (in sequence of joining): Hongkong Land, Zall Holdings, Shanghai Stater Investment Holdings, Tianyi Holdings, Tongxin Real Estate, Tusincere Group, China Resources Land, Nash Work, Nan Fung Investment China Holdings, Topchain Group, Jiaming Investment, Ronald Lu & Partners. The consortium members supported our field work and research workshops, but had no direct influence on the research findings and views expressed in this book.

The volume editors and authors of this book declare that there is no conflict of interest.

About the MIT Sustainable Urbanization Lab (SUL)

The predecessor of SUL at MIT is the China Future City Lab (CFC) founded by Siqi Zheng and Zhengzhen Tan in November 2017. China's unprecedented urbanization wave has not only changed the lives of hundreds of millions but also modified the world's political, economic, social and environmental landscapes. CFC aimed to contribute to understanding the demand for and supply of key urban policies and innovations in an emerging market—in China's case, one with strong state control.

We are now extending our analytic framework and research approach to the most rapidly urbanizing regions of the world. With this expansion of focal areas to include a broader set of countries and cities—including but not exclusive to China—in December 2019 we renamed the lab the Sustainable Urbanization Lab (SUL). Our overarching goal as a research lab is to establish the behavioral and economic foundations for urban and environmental planning and policies aimed at sustainable urbanization; and connect our research with urbanization and real estate industry leaders, entrepreneurs, and policy makers to generate real impacts on the ground.

The SUL organizes its work around three interrelated research themes: Environmental Sustainability; Place-Based Policies and Self-Sustaining Urban Growth; and the China Future City Program (an educational program that will continue to serve as the teaching and research center of China's urbanization at MIT). *Toward Urban Economic Vibrancy: Patterns and Practices of Asia's New Cities* is a project under the "place-based policies and self-sustaining urban growth" theme.

For more information of MIT Sustainable Urbanization Lab, visit: https://www.sul.mit.edu/

Editors

Siqi Zheng, Samuel Tak Lee Associate Professor, Department of Urban Studies and Planning, and Center for Real Estate; Faculty Director, Sustainable Urbanization Lab, Massachusetts Institute of Technology

Zhengzhen Tan, Lecturer, Department of Urban Studies and Planning, and Center for Real Estate; Executive Director, Sustainable Urbanization Lab, Massachusetts Institute of Technology

Authors

Colleen Chiu-Shee, PhD candidate, Department of Urban Studies and Planning, Massachusetts Institute of Technology

Victor Jansson, Director of Industrial, JLL East China

Angie Jo, PhD student, Department of Political Science, Massachusetts Institute of Technology

Matthew E. Kahn, Bloomberg Distinguished Professor of Economics and Business, Johns Hopkins University; and Research Associate, NBER.

Manish Srivastava, Visiting Associate Professor, Massachusetts Institute of Technology; Clinical Associate Professor, New York University; Visiting Professor, SDA Bocconi School of Management, Milan, Italy

Weizeng Sun, Associate Professor, Central University of Finance and Economics, China

Ningdi Wei, Associate Director, Administrative Committee of Zhengdong New District, China

Jianfeng Wu, Associate Professor, China Center for Economic Studies (CCES) & Shanghai-Hongkong Development Institute (SHKDI), Fudan University; Senior research fellow, Shanghai Institute of International Finance and Economics, China

Wingshan Yip, PhD student, Hang Lung Center for Real Estate and Department of Construction Management, Tsinghua University, China

Yicheng Zhao, Junior research associate, Shanghai-Hongkong Development Institute (SHKDI), Fudan University, China

Introduction

Siqi Zheng, Zhengzhen Tan[1]

Urbanization and New Cities in Asia

Asia has experienced a dramatic urbanization process over the past few decades. Nearly half of the 4 billion residents of developing Asia lived in urban areas in 2017 (Asian Development Bank 2019). Another 1 billion or more are projected to join them in the next 30 years, pushing the regional urbanization rate over 64% by 2050. The rapid urbanization trend has reshaped Asian economies as cities generate agglomeration economies—reducing the cost of moving goods, services, people, and knowledge; enabling workers and firms to interact in close physical proximity; allowing specialization; and nurturing entrepreneurship. Urbanized Asia has become a global powerhouse, generating more than one third of the world's total GDP.

One significant urbanization trend across Asian countries is the widespread prevalence of "new planned cities" (new cities, hereafter), where public or private actors have the power to assemble large areas of land for new development from scratch. In recent decades the new cities building boom has taken place across Asia (in China, India, South Korea, Malaysia, Indonesia, etc.) as well as other fast-growing regions in the whole world (in the United Arab Emirates, Saudi Arabia, etc.). In terms of sheer volume, China is undoubtedly the global front of this new city boom. If we consider large industrial parks as the seeds of new, so-called consumption cities that develop around them, we see that China has built 1,568 national-level and provincial-level industrial parks in 270 municipalities since 1998, which account for about 10% of China's GDP and 33% of its foreign direct investment (Zheng et al. 2017). In another study, scholars have manually collected data on at least 675 new towns launched between 2000 and 2014 in over 270 municipalities across the country, which collectively cover over 66,000 sq. km (Chang and Lu 2017). The master plans of those new cities address not only their physical form, but also their economic development strategy. Whether the role of the "central planner" (or "central coordinator") of a new city is fulfilled by a public actor (government entity) or a private actor (e.g., a powerful developer or conglomerate), it is evident that those central planners explicitly conceptualize these projects primarily as long-term investments for *urban economic vibrancy*.

The boom of new cities in Asia can be traced through the interaction of both internal and external forces associated with local, industrial upgrading. At the early stage, these new cities were notable for their geographical location at a city's edge as well as for their creation around industrial parks. Many Asian cities confronted incessant rural-urban migration that generated a strong, urgent demand for urban space and attendant basic urban services. At the same time, foreign investors tended to seek business opportunities in, and outsource their production activities to, Asian

1. We acknowledge Jianfeng Wu's helpful contribution to this introduction piece.

cities to take advantage of cheaper land and labor. The interplay of both internal and external forces prompted many Asian cities to engage in global production and distribution chains. To attract those investments, many Asian city governments started to build industrial parks, around 50 to 100 km from the city center. These industrial parks attracted industrial activities to concentrate spatially, and then consumption activities followed, eventually evolving into one of the subcenters in the city. Such new cities developed from industrial parks have been prevalent in China and Southeast Asia since the beginning of the 1980s.

Those industrial parks allowed Asian economies to accumulate great wealth and skills, providing them with opportunities to finance housing and infrastructure to support the growing concentration of people and activities. One of the recent ambitious programs of Asian mayors is to restructure their cities' economies by upgrading the industrial structure, strategically targeting technology and high-end service sectors, so as to maintain their cities' competitiveness in the global economy. To accommodate these new economic activities, these city governments have poured huge investments into building new cities at the edges of core areas, with special land, tax, financial, and economic policies to recruit highly productive firms. Such new cities, characterized by their multiple live-work-play functions include shopping centers, R&D centers, government agencies, residences, and transportation hubs.

Physical proximity among firms who seek to co-agglomerate facilitates local, economic growth through stimulating trade by lowering transportation costs and by facilitating learning and social interaction. Moreover, these new cities stimulate economic growth by solving a land-assembly problem and a cross-firm coordination problem and allowing firms to form clusters in a timely fashion, thanks to the top-down, place-based policies. These benefits are more difficult to reap in those cities that feature pre-existing durable structures and bottom-up decentralized decision-making context (Zheng et al. 2017).

This new generation of planned cities has yet to receive much theoretical or empirical scholarship. Scholars in the fields of global urban studies, critical urban theory, urban planning, and urban geography have so far been critical. Critics fear that developers seek only to buy greenfield land at low prices and sell luxury properties at much higher prices; vendor firms to sell their tech products while the "smart city" trend is hot; local governments to capture one-time windfalls in fiscal revenue by selling land to the highest bidder; and politicians to stimulate construction booms that temporarily improve their political standing, no matter the actual utility of what they are building, and eventually lead to many aptly called "ghost towns" (see chapter 1). What this critical view does not consider, however, is whether there are also ways in which new planned cities can create new, broader economic and societal value—through coordinated concentration by solving market failures, generating positive externalities, unlocking innovation, or opening up new sectors—and how unique, public-private planning processes may be necessary to produce these desirable outcomes. This positive view is discussed by economists who regard new planned cities as a prominent "place-based policy." They point out the upside of creating agglomeration economies and internalizing positive externalities, as well as the downside of possible capital misallocation (Duranton and Venables 2018).

This book is an intervention into the evolving debate about new cities in Asia. It seeks to understand the economic vibrancy of these new cities in Asia and underlying driving forces. A close examination of some representative, new city cases in four Asian economies—China, South Korea, India, and Malaysia—provides us vivid on-the-ground stories of how those new cities' economies have experienced.

Urban Economic Vibrancy of New Cities

We use the concept of *urban economic vibrancy*, or *urban vibrancy* in short, to refer to the size, density, and diversity of urban agglomeration economies, including production and consumption agglomerations. We evaluate the *urban vibrancy performance* of new cities in Asia, especially in China, since the 1990s. The central planners of these new cities, whether local government entities or private developers (or partnerships between them), regard achieving a vibrant urban economy as one of their most important goals as they build new cities. They use creative strategies to attract to their new cities productive and innovative firms as well as talented workers. Urban vibrancy complements the more general review of new cities in Asia by sharpening the economic analysis of building new cities at the interactions between economic mechanisms, urban financing systems and digital transformation.

Toward Urban Economic Vibrancy: Patterns and Practices in Asia's New Cities examines the forces generating new cities' economic vibrancy from three perspectives: 1) the economic mechanisms that foster dense and diverse production and consumption activities; 2) the creative financing models; 3) and the role of transformational digital urban systems in enhancing urban vibrancy in the context of new economy.

The first perspective involves increasing the size, density, and diversity of production and consumption activities. Business will be more productive and profitable in a dense area as it benefits from agglomeration economies, input sharing, and knowledge spillovers from both its own sector and other industries. Individuals are also likely to be more productive and enjoy high levels of well-being when they live in dense and diversified areas thanks to job-market matching and learning opportunities. It is thus vital for a new city to foster agglomeration economies by creating incentives for firms and people to relocate, and thus to stimulate investment, job creation, entrepreneurship, and innovation.

The second perspective is to develop a self-sustaining, financing system for new cities. Financial health is an important issue for a new city to support its vibrancy. To attract industrial activities and foster population growth, a new city needs to build and maintain infrastructure systems and public buildings, offer affordable housing, and provide goods and services for the public. Devising a feasible and self-sustaining financial model is, therefore, of great significance in supporting the development of new cities. In fact, building a new city needs a huge influx of money upfront; both private investors and city governments need to finance these projects using various financial vehicles including land sale/leasing, loans, and bonds. These new cities take great financial risks, because their failure to create a vibrant economy would mean not generating the cash flows needed to repay their heavy debts.

A third perspective relates to digital technology. This stage of technological innovation will be transformational to urban development in three dimensions: the first is to increase operational efficiency of urban systems; the second is to improve integrated, user experience of public and private city services; the third is to develop new business models for both public and private city services. Digital urban systems play a bigger role in urban vibrancy in the new economy and have sustaining impact in the planning, design, development and operation of new cities.

Toward Urban Economic Vibrancy: Patterns and Practices in Asia's New Cities examines and assesses the performance of new cities with a particular focus on China given the huge volume and high intensity of new city boom there. China has the largest urban population in Asia and has achieved rapid progress in urbanization; it has averaged a one percent growth rate since the beginning of 1980s. More importantly, China's urbanization has been promoted not only by the market incentives but also by government efforts. The governments at both the central and local levels have proactively led this change by acquiring land, building new cities, and investing in infrastructure. The success or failure of such a top-down initiative, as they interact with bottom-up market forces, will have a long-lasting effect on China's economy or even the whole Asia.

Other Asian countries have also embraced the idea of building new cities to enliven their urban-based economies. Some of them have achieved great economic vibrancy by attracting high-end services, innovation, and entrepreneurship activities. They differ from new city projects in China as most of them were initiated by local governments and invested in by private investors. Highlighting the performance of those projects and the driving forces of urban vibrancy can enrich our understanding of new city developments throughout Asia.

Structure of this Book

Despite the great interest governments, developers, and media have shown in the potential of new planned cities, they are insufficiently studied in academia. Two books, one by Daniels, Ho, and Hutton (2012) and the other by Provoost and Vanstiphout (2011), have made worthwhile contributions. As Percival & Waley (2012) note, "while these projects are beginning to receive academic attention, the majority of studies have a limited capacity to explain why and how they are produced." This is particularly true of the new cities' economic rationale: policy makers and scholars alike often leave unexplained how exactly these projects are designed to deliver returns on investment—in what form, with what likelihood of success, under what conditions, and to whose accrual (see Chapter 1).

In Chapter 1, we lay out our conceptual framework to understand the global trend in building new cities. Chapters 2 through 7 mainly focus on China. Chapters 8 and 9 present case studies in other Asian countries: Malaysia, India, and South Korea. Quantitative assessment methods are used to examine new city patterns in China, given the availability of both China and micro-level data there. A case-study approach is used when studying new cities in other Asian countries.

In Chapter 1, Angie Jo and Siqi Zheng outline the high-level conceptual framework under which our book project examines the global trend in building new cities and the contemporary new planned cities in general. Their framework emphasizes the key role of centralized coordination (rather than control) of market and non-market resources that marks this new model of new city planning. They then delineate the critical decisions that the central coordinators of a new city project must make during the planning process—the where, what, and when—in order to maximize its long-term economic development prospects. Finally, they also briefly discuss both the new opportunities and the associated risks that this model of new city planning raises.

In Chapter 2 Jianfeng Wu and Yicheng Zhao present a quantitative approach to measure cities' economic vibrancy in China. They first present the evolution of economic geography of the new cities across prefectural-level cities in China since the beginning of the 1990s. Then they employ a ternary method to identify the performance of these new city samples in terms of urban vibrancy, measured as the composite indicator of built-up area, population density, and the density of economic activity. They also explore the key determinants of the big variation in urban vibrancy across these new cities.

In Chapter 3, Siqi Zheng, Weizeng Sun, Jianfeng Wu, and Matthew Kahn present the economic vibrancy model of industrial parks, a typical type of new cities in China. Such new cities evolved from the establishment of industrial parks, fashioned by both central and local governments to promote urban industrial development and economic growth. The authors document the economic mechanisms according to which an urban "edge city" is created from a manufacturing-oriented industrial park. They argue that such a new city arises from the clustering of both vibrant production and consumption activities around an established industrial park.

In Chapter 4, Manish Srivastava and Wingshan Yip analyze the urban vibrancy of new cities in China from the perspective of their financing models. These two authors introduce the historical evolution of financing new cities in China and discuss newly developed financing tools and the way ahead. They also analyze the potential risks associated with different financing vehicles for new cities development.

In Chapter 5, Zhengzhen Tan hypothesizes a framework for the transformational changes that digital technology will play in promoting urban vibrancy in the future generation of new cities. Compared to the digital transformation of existing cities, new planned digital cities may provide a faster and more sustainable way to achieve economic vibrancy in the coming decade.

Chapter 6 and 7 present two prominent new city cases in China. The new city case in Chapter 6, written by Colleen Chiu-Shee, Ningdi Wei and Siqi Zheng, is the government-led Zhengdong New District in Zhengzhou city. It is one of the pioneers of China's new cities development. In its early stage its high vacancy rate was widely criticized, but after two decades' development, it is now regarded as one of China's most economically vibrant new cities. In Chapter 7 Angie Jo presents a case study of Gu'An New Industry City, which is the most representative new city invested in and developed by a publicly listed new city developer, China Fortune Land Development (CFLD), with its unique "public-private partnership" (PPP) model.

In the last two chapters, we employ our analytical framework to examine some new city cases in other Asian countries. Victor Jansson led the research on new cities in Malaysia and India. The two cases in Malaysia are Cyberjaya, a city driven by industry promotion and development, and Iskandar Puteri, a city taking advantage of its proximity to the city-country of Singapore. The new city case in India is Atal Nagar, which was invested in and driven by its local government. Angie Jo worked on the South Korean experience in developing new cities, using Pangyo new city as a case. Pangyo is one of the few successful cases of cluster formation directed by a local government in South Korea, and its 3.3 km^2 area is now a home to some of Korea's brightest young companies and corporate consortia.

References

Asian Development Bank. 2019. *Asian Development Outlook 2019 Update: Fostering Growth and Inclusion in Asia's Cities*. Asian Development Bank. http://dx.doi.org/10.22617/FLS190445-3.

Chang, Chen, and Ming Lu. 2017. "Misery of New Town—Density, Distance and Debt." *China Economic Quarterly*, no. 4: 16.

Daniels, Peter W., Kong-Chong Ho, and Thomas A. Hutton. 2012. *New Economic Spaces in Asian Cities: From Industrial Restructuring to the Cultural Turn*. Taylor & Francis.

Duranton, Gilles, and Anthony J Venables. 2018. "Place-Based Policies for Development." *NBER Working Paper No. 24562*, April. https://doi.org/10.3386/w24562.

Percival, Tom, and Paul Waley. 2012. "Articulating Intra-Asian Urbanism: The Production of Satellite Cities in Phnom Penh." *Urban Studies* 49 (13): 2873–2888.

Provoost, and Vanstiphout. 2011. "Introduction Chapter." In *Rising in the East: Contemporary New Towns in Asia*. International New Town Institute, SUN.

Zheng, Siqi, Weizeng Sun, Jianfeng Wu, and Matthew E. Kahn. 2017. "The Birth of Edge Cities in China: Measuring the Effects of Industrial Parks Policy." *Journal of Urban Economics* 100: 80–103.

Chapter 1.

New Planned Cities as Economic Engines: Global Trend and Our Conceptual Framework

Angie Jo, Siqi Zheng[1]

Introduction

In recent years scholars and journalists have observed a global resurgence of "new cities" planned and built from scratch over the past two decades (Keeton 2011; Moser 2015; Shepard 2017). While there is no consensus on what "new," "planned" or even "city" means universally, it appears true that a broad class of large-scale development projects has emerged with roughly the following features:[2]

Master-planned and project managed by a "central planner" – Major decisions and factor investments (e.g. land assembly, infrastructure, industry types to recruit) are made in advance by a few primary actors, usually subnational governments in public-private partnerships, but in some cases, by private sector real estate developers and investors.

Rapidly built in a coordinated fashion – The project follows construction, population, and job creation sequences under the scope of a single coordinated project, rather than growing in piecemeal over time.

Built on greenfield – The land had little or no built-up urban fabric (e.g. rural land, land reclaimed from the sea, released greenbelt zones, state-owned or -expropriated land).

Distinct from other urban settlements – The project has geographic, fiscal, administrative, and conceptual separation from developed areas in existing cities (i.e. not an urban renewal or expansion zone).

Pre-determined, multi-functional mix of uses – The project is intended for both consumption and production functions (i.e. neither solely a bedroom-town nor a pure cluster of jobs), and has a mix of industrial, residential and commercial activities that generate both tradable (e.g. IT, government, manufacturing) and non-tradable jobs (e.g. restaurants, retail, janitorial).

Explicitly envisioned as a "city" by its creators — The project is designed not merely as a large, gated residential community, commercial complex, science park, university campus, resort, or transit hub (though it may include those things), but rather, as a holistic urban environment where people "live, work, play," and reside "from cradle to grave."[3]

---

1. We are grateful to the valuable comments and suggestions we received from Amy Glasmeier, Bish Sanyal, Jason Jackson, Brent Ryan, Yasheng Huang, Ming Lu, Charlie Xue, Yongheng Yang, Shouying Liu, Kui Feng, Sam Youl Lee, Park Baegyoon, Zhengzhen Tan, the participants at the "MIT China New City Forum" in November 2018 in Beijing, and the participants at the "IDG Development Studies Seminar" at MIT Department of Urban Studies and Planning in April 2019.

2. This working definition draws from fieldwork conducted by journalists and field researchers such as Wade Shepard (2018). Other scholars and practitioners use terms such as "new town," "satellite city," and "urban integrated mega project" to describe more and less similar projects.

3. Of course, simply calling a newly developed mega-project a new city—often as part of branding strategy for selling real estate property within it—does not make it one. However, it is worth noting that the planners of these projects intentionally evoke the scale, density, multi-functionality, and variety of experiences often associated with the "urban," even as it comes with potentially greater costs and challenges above their experience in real estate.

Emerging research, press, and media suggest the widespread prevalence of such projects in many countries of the Global South, concentrated in regions where public or private actors have the power to assemble large areas of land for development, as in parts of India, Southeast Asia, the Gulf Coast states and Middle East, and throughout Africa.[4] In terms of sheer volume, however, China is undoubtedly the global fount of new city planning and building activity. A state survey conducted in just twelve out of China's thirty-two provinces found over 200 active "new town" projects under development as of 2013, and the national total is likely double or triple that number.[5] If we consider large industrial parks as the seeds for new "consumption cities" that develop around them, we see that China has built 1,568 national-level and provincial-level industrial parks in 270 municipalities since 1998, which account for about 10% of China's GDP and 33% of its foreign direct investment (Kahn et al. 2018). Separately from official numbers, scholars in China have manually collected data on at least 675 new towns launched between 2000 and 2014 in over 270 municipalities across the country, which collectively cover over 66,000 km^2 —an area larger than Sri Lanka (Chang and Lu 2017). And while these projects are often described as new "towns" or "districts" within the Chinese administrative lexicon, the average new city is about 115 km^2 in size, has a density of 8,000 people per km^2, and is located 25 km away from its nearest neighbouring city (Chang and Lu 2017). Thus even allowing for definitional debates, this intensive planning and building activity is not a fringe phenomenon, but a distinctive process by which urbanization is occurring today. In this particular sense, the world is becoming not only more urban but perhaps also more "planned."

Departing from precedents in the past—new cities planned primarily as political and bureaucratic capitals, such as Brasilia and Chandigarh; residential New Town movements in England, Hong Kong, and Singapore; or industrial cities built under the command economies of the Soviet Union and socialist China—the proposed function of most contemporary, new city projects is to serve as new economic engines in today's so-called "knowledge economy." Planners and governments assert that creating new cities will allow them to enter higher-skill sectors, trigger creative clusters and innovation hubs, and competitively attract valuable workers, firms, and investment to their region above other regions, and ultimately, stimulate their local economic growth. In many cases, new cities are explicitly considered an engine for local economic growth and a medium for industrial policy. For example, King Abdullah Economic City (KAEC) and four other "economic cities" under

4. For examples in India, see Datta (2015) and Datta and Shaban (2016); in Southeast Asia, see Rizzo and Glasson (2012), Dieleman (2011), Bunnell et al.(2013)and Douglass and Huang (2007); in the Gulf Coast states and Middle East, see Tok et al. (2015), Al-Filali and Gallarotti (2012), Moser, Swain, and Alkhabbaz (2015), and Rizzo (2017); and Africa, see Watson (2014), Herbert and Murray (2015), and Van Noorloos and Kloosterboer (2018).
5. National Development and Reform Commission, qtd. in Yin, Liu, and Wang (2018).

construction in Saudi Arabia are intended to diversify the kingdom away from its reliance on crude oil, provide one million new jobs, and "leapfrog into a post-oil knowledge economy" (Moser, Swain, and Alkhabbaz 2015). Dholera Industry City in Gujarat, India—the prototype of Prime Minister Modi's campaign to build 100 new smart cities—is also supposed to create 800,000 jobs, house two million inhabitants by 2040 and generate long-term economic growth as "the building blocks of global Gujarat," in Modi's words.[6]

But despite the great interest shown by governments and developers in their potential, this new generation of planned cities has yet to receive much theoretical or empirical scholarship. As geographers Percival and Waley note, "while these projects are beginning to receive academic attention, the majority of studies have a limited capacity to explain why and how they are produced." (Percival and Waley 2012). This is particularly true of their economic rationale: policy makers and scholars alike often leave unexplained how exactly these projects are designed to deliver returns on investment—in what form, with what likelihood of success, under what conditions, and to whose accrual. As Moser observes, "there is a widespread view that new cities are a crucial part of any emerging economy's toolkit for economic growth, yet very little research has been conducted to determine the extent to which this is true" (Shepard 2017).

Existing scholarship on new planned cities in global urban studies, critical urban theory, and geography has so far taken a critical view of these projects, especially of the increasing involvement of private sector firms and real estate developers in their development. Critics emphasize the "explicitly profit-oriented and commodified nature" of these projects (Shatkin 2011) and trace their impetus to "the corporate sector seeking to create new global markets" (Datta 2015). Moser argues that corporations are the new colonizers, so to speak: transnational firms like Cisco, IBM, and McKinsey are the "descendants of and heirs to colonial imperial city building," now enabled by "the spread of neo-liberal ideology that brings state and national governments into close collaboration with corporations". (Moser 2015) Put simply, these critiques express the concern that the principal agents involved in planning new cities—subnational governments, national politicians, private real estate developers, tech companies, and consulting firms—will use new cities solely as opportunities to extract their own zero-sum gains in the short term, rather than creating positive-sum value for society in the long term. Critics fear that developers seek only to buy greenfield land low and sell luxury properties high; vendor firms seek only to sell their tech products while the "smart city" trend is hot; local governments seek only to capture one-time windfalls in fiscal revenue by selling land to the highest bidder; and politicians seek only to stimulate construction booms that temporarily improve

6. Halcrow Group, qtd. in Ayona Datta (2015).

their political standing, no matter the actual utility of what they are building.

However, what this critical view does not consider is whether there are also ways in which new planned cities can create new, broader economic and societal *value*—through coordinated concentration (compared to the "counterfactual scenario" where those economic activities happened in other places and those resources were dispersed)—by solving market failures, generating positive externalities, unlocking innovation, or opening up new sectors—and how unique public-private planning processes may be necessary to produce these desirable outcomes.

Urban economists, for example, have found that Chinese industrial parks—special economic zones that use financial incentives to cluster complementary manufacturing facilities, about 1500 of which have been built by the state since the 1990s—generate significant positive productivity gain within the parks as well as "spillover" benefits to their local regions in about 70% of cases (Zheng et al. 2017). Firms in the vicinity of the park tend to be more productive and residents tend to consume more, leading to the development of new "edge cities" surrounding the initial industrial cores. Industrial parks are also associated with a 20% increase in municipal GDP ten years after their launch (Alder, Shao, and Zilibotti 2016). These examples illustrate how centralized planning and public-private collaboration, in both the urban and industrial domains, have the potential to trigger positive externalities and productivity gains that would not have otherwise arisen on their own.

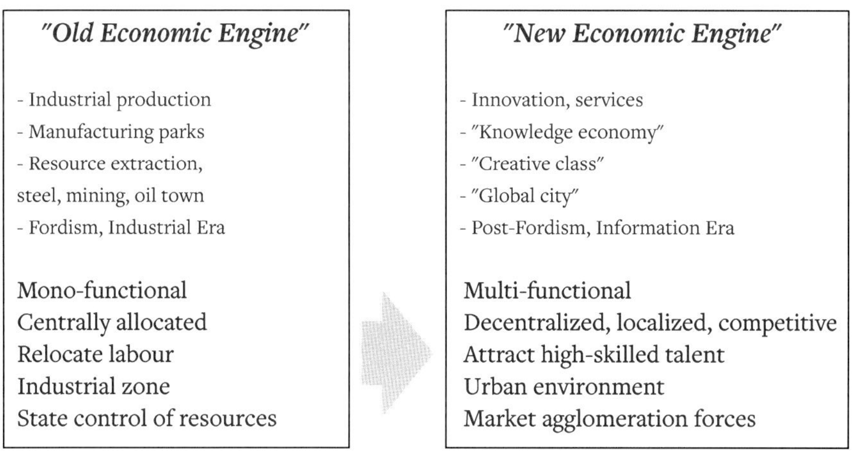

Figure 1.1: Shifts in the intended economic function of planned cities

New cities that are designed to be new economic engines might be thought of as evolutions of industrial parks. Yet their complexity as *cities*—which must competitively attract high-skill, knowledge-intensive firms, workers, and residents in the free market using their *economic and urban vibrancy*—distinguishes them from the pure clusters of jobs and planned industrial cities of old. New cities are multifunctional, not monofunctional; they are not just sites of production, but sites of production and consumption; they are neither purely residential nor purely industrial but must offer the full range of urban amenities. For, unlike industrial workers who followed factory work wherever production costs were lowest, the highly educated "talent" that work in the knowledge economy—a highly desirable workforce for local governments—tend to vote with their feet: they demand cities that allow them to maintain a high quality of life while being close to their jobs (a "live-work-play" lifestyle), as well as raise their families in clean, consumer-friendly, vibrant, urban environments unpolluted by heavy industries.

A shift in the intended economic function of new cities—and in the firms, workers, and residents that they are now designed to attract—has required public and private planners to use a new model of city-making. The old model that relied on state *control* over non-market resources such as land, taxes, and infrastructure—used by governments throughout history to build cities for political, social, and industrial purposes—could certainly still be used to build out all the physical structures of a new city, exactly according to an urban masterplan. But it could not guarantee that people would voluntarily come to live, work, or play in it once it was built. State control cannot be used to induce the urban and economic *vibrancy* that governments now want out of new cities. This transformation thus also calls for a new conceptual framework to understand the purpose, planning, and performance of new cities as new economic engines, as well as the new interactions between state and market that they bring about.

In this paper, we outline the high-level conceptual framework under which we are pursuing a broad research project on contemporary new planned cities. First, we emphasize the key role of centralized *coordination*—rather than *control*—of market and non-market resources that marks this new model of new city planning. Importantly, we argue that there is a rationale for the increased involvement of private actors and public-private partnerships in this process, as well as potential for increased value and vibrancy from their involvement. Second, we delineate the critical decisions that the central coordinators of a new city project must make during the planning process—the *where*, *what*, and *when*—in order to maximize its long-term economic development prospects. We draw from interviews with both government officials and prominent private developers who have led public and public-private projects (primarily in China), and illuminate their internal perspectives as planners who face difficult decisions without much *ex ante* knowledge to guide them. Third, we briefly discuss both the new opportunities and new risks that this model of new city planning raises.

The Key Role of Coordination (vs. Control)

In economics research, planned cities can be understood through the framework of place-based policies (PBPs) in development economics. Place-based policies are subsidies or investments that target specific geographic areas and are allocated in a top-down manner by the state (Neumark and Simpson 2015; Duranton and Venables 2018; Glaeser and Gottlieb 2008). In contrast to "people-based policies" that apply regardless of geography (for example, welfare benefits for low-income citizens), place-based policies are intended to strengthen a specific region's economy by leveraging its spatial qualities. PBPs typically include transportation infrastructure, such as highways, high-speed rail, and subway networks; preferential business areas, such as special economic zones, enterprise/empowerment zones, or tax-exempt areas; and urban amenities, such as renewed housing stock.

Building a new city might be thought of as analogous to a government sinking an enormous bundle of all the possible PBPs they can muster (large assembled land, utilities and infrastructure, transportation networks, preferential business policies, new housing stock, subsidized industrial land, government-controlled jobs, as well as public entities like civic and cultural centers) into a place where there was previously nothing. This is a function of state *control* over non-market resources: if a state has a high degree of control, it can move and concentrate resources effectively and in a timely fashion, and trigger a transformation from an empty greenfield expanse to a new political capital, a new military fortress city, a new residential town, a new steel or factory town, or industrial park in a matter of years.

Of course, the obvious weakness of a city-making model that relies on state control of resources is its lack of market logic. Place-based policies, by definition, require expensive and contentious trade-offs among location choices—if region A receives these benefits, region B does not. If region A is weaker than region B, it may stand to benefit the most from receiving these investments from an equity perspective; however, if region A is too weak for secondary investment, firms, and workers to follow and flourish after the public investments and subsidies are sunk, the high opportunity costs of those investments are an argument for spending them on region B instead. There are complex and dynamic "spatial general equilibrium" effects triggered by such top-down policies, and the accurate estimation of such effects is still a big challenge facing economists. What is more, central planners must also take into account broader market trends, timing, and the existing factor endowments and fundamentals of each region, in order to determine what kinds of investments and economic activities would enjoy the most synergy in which places.

These are extremely difficult decisions for any central planner to make because they have little knowledge *ex ante* of what PBPs and industrial policies make the most sense in each region, and they lack the immediate feedback of market pressures. For example, even though Chinese state-directed industrial parks produced positive spillover in the majority of cases, about 30% of them failed to do so—which means nearly one in three projects created this way turned out to be a waste of resources: they turned into "ghost parks" full of buildings and roads but not people (Zheng et al. 2017). In addition, cronyism—whereby politicians gift scarce resources, such as multi-billion dollar industrial parks, to the municipalities where their friends hold office—partly explains these misallocations (Kahn et al. 2018). Such weaknesses of state-led model of new city-making—through its *control* over bundles of place-based policies—are thus not just ineffective but also possibly very harmful in causing pure losses in social welfare.

That said, on the other end of the planning vs. markets spectrum a new economic engine in the form of a new city would not materialize out of thin air either if the market were left to its own devices. While a market-led model faces less risk of resource misallocation, market actors suffer from a *coordination* problem. High density clusters of firms generate positive externalities; these economies enjoy higher productivity from agglomeration. This is the external benefit that individual firms can create for their neighboring firms when they locate together. However, because firms and workers make location decisions based on individual cost-benefit analyses—not based on potential benefits from collective action—it is difficult for distributed firms to collectively decide to co-locate and form a new cluster, even if they all stand to gain from doing so. The market equilibrium density will therefore be lower than the socially optimal density, which leads to a loss in efficiency for the whole society. And even if market actors recognize these benefits, they also suffer from a "first mover" problem: no individual firm volunteers to bear the disproportionate cost of trying to coordinate across firms, and nobody wants to take the risk of being the first to move to a new cluster or a new city without the guarantee that others will follow. And even if such cross-firm coordination were to take place, such a coalition of firms would still need to front enormous capital resources, either to carve out an area within an existing city to house their new cluster—the prospect of which is highly implausible in cities with pre-existing urban fabric and 'Not In My Back Yard' opposition—or to acquire enough greenfield land to build out their own new city from scratch, in which case they would inevitably require the intervention, approval, or involvement of the state.[7] In short, individual firms in the market lack the motive and mechanisms to collectively provide such public goods by themselves.

A useful analogy to illustrate this coordination problem is the suburban shopping mall.[8] The idea is that each individual store wanting to operate in the suburbs would

---

7. The recent experiences of the "seasteading" movement—which attempts to create permanent "floating" settlements on the high seas outside any sovereign territories—illustrate the difficulties faced by private market actors in trying to form a new urban agglomeration of their own, entirely without state support or involvement.
8. Originally referenced in Zheng et al., (2017)

prefer to be in an agglomeration with other stores—a shopping mall—over being on its own. Being in a mall produces positive externalities for all the stores inside it by virtue of spatial concentration: capturing a convenience premium by lowering consumers' search and travel costs ("one-stop shopping"); saving on shared overhead costs such as maintenance, advertising, and public facilities; learning new product ideas and strategies from being in close proximity with rivals; and enjoying lower prices for auxiliary services that can serve all the stores in bulk. In particular, small stores benefit from the presence of large anchor stores (such as Macy's, Costco, Home Depot, etc.) that draw many customers. And yet no one store would volunteer to coordinate all the stores in the suburbs to start a new mall, or take the risk of being the first store to move into an empty mall complex without a guarantee that other stores will join them. Given this situation, the owner of the shopping mall is incentivized to take on the task of coordinating among stores. The owner recruits stores to its new mall by assuring them they would be moving in together with other attractive neighbouring stores, and in a top-down manner, arranges them in optimal spatial formations to maximize customer traffic and sales (for example, by making sure a gym, a smoothie shop, and a Nike store are located next to each other). In particular, they solve the "first mover" problem by first offering subsidized rent to the large anchor stores.[9] If these "big fish" bite and agree to move into the mall, given the lower location costs, the owner can then use their presence as a bargaining chip to recruit the "small fish" to the mall as well. If, through the shopping mall owner's actions as a coordinator, the mall becomes more than the sum of its parts—that is, if the stores enjoy more sales in the mall than if the same stores were dispersed throughout the suburbs—the owner is compensated for their coordination services via a premium in rent revenue from their tenants.

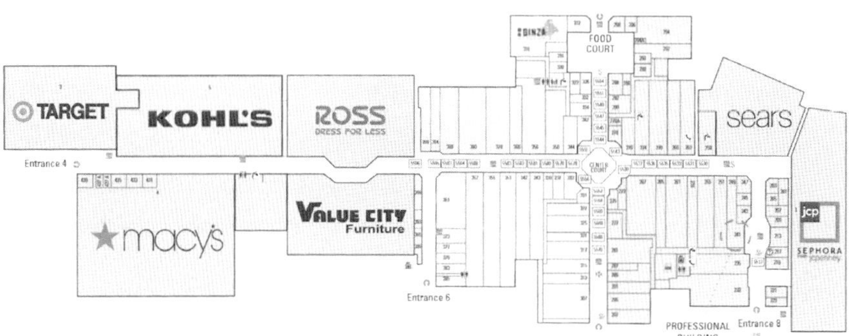

Figure 1.2: The «shopping mall» as an analogy for recruiting firms to a new planned city
Source: Jo (2019)

9. This phenomenon is shown empirically in Pashigian and Gould (1998) and Gould, Pashigian, and Prendergast (2005).

Similarly, central *coordination* is key to the formation of a new planned city. The planner and central coordinator of this new city has the potential to create more than the sum of the parts—both in terms of non-market resources (land, infrastructure, subsidies) and free-moving market actors (firms, workers, private investment)—by acting like "shopping mall owners." They can solve land assembly problems, build out foundational infrastructure, and provide credible signals for the future prospects of the new city—by announcing, for example, the priority industries that the city will specialize in, publicizing project timelines and targets, and building out prominent public goods, such as public green spaces. Setting these expectations and illustrating the long-term vision for the new city is critical, because location choices for both firms and households are major decisions involving large sunk costs and long time horizons. In addition, the central coordinator can use its industrial and commercial networks to recruit productive firms from its prioritized sectors, starting with "big fish" to reel in "small fish," or negotiating package move-in deals between many complementary entities at once to maximize synergy (for example, a biomedical hub that combines a consortium of bio-tech firms with a national hospital and public research institute for life sciences).

In other words, in order to build a successful new city—one that will act as a new economic engine in today's knowledge economy—there needs to be a convergence of many elements: state control of non-market resources (place-based policies), investment and industrial policies that align with market logic (which attracts free-moving firms and workers), and most importantly, coordination among all of these resources (the work of a "shopping mall owner"). The role of the central coordinator provides a set of valuable services that neither the state (susceptible to misallocation failures) nor the aggregate of individual market actors (susceptible to coordination

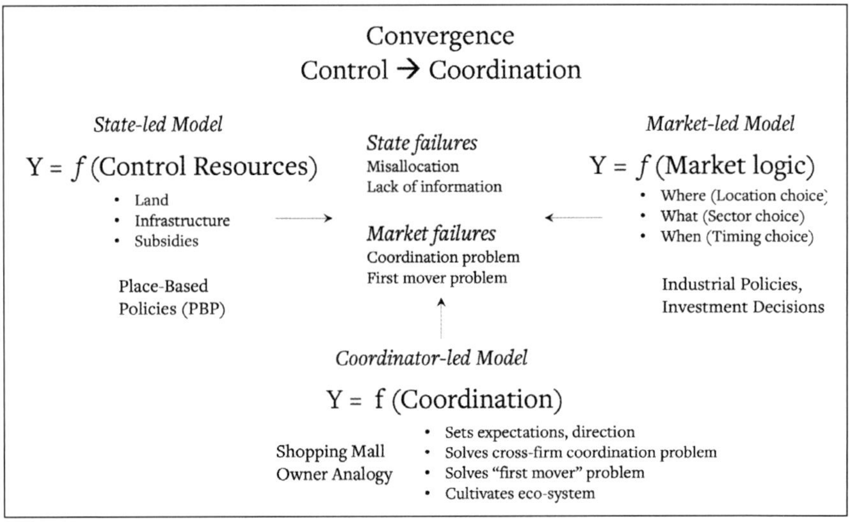

Figure 1.3: The role of centralized coordination in planning new cities

failures) have access to on their own.

This added value is what theoretically justifies the increased involvement of entrepreneurs from the private sector—such as private real estate developers, the real estate and investment branches of diversified business groups and conglomerates, or even large technology firms at the center of innovation ecosystems—to play the role of "private planners" for new cities. In particular, weak governments with low capacity may seek strong partners in the private sector to undertake this coordination work on their behalf, including tasks in comprehensive urban development, industrial research and policy expertise, and corporate recruitment. As in the case of Gu'an New Industry City (see Chapter 7)—which was planned through a public-private partnership between a weak county government and a strong private developer, China Fortune Land Development—governments can explicitly structure these arrangements into multi-decade contracts that tie the profits of the private planner to the long-term economic health and growth of the new city.

In China, private real estate developers are now entering these new markets by acquiring expertise in technology and industry development. Developers face difficulty winning land in competitive auctions otherwise: local governments reportedly refuse to grant developers the lease rights to build lucrative residential properties unless they come combined with a high-end industrial development component, even though industrial zones are lower-margin products for developers. As one developer put it, "the rise of technology allows private developers to get more involved with non-traditional real estate business, because that's what local governments want expertise in. Governments that start new city projects all want technology such as bio-tech, eco-tech, etc., which are more likely to attract residents and companies. Developers who have that expertise can out-compete traditional developers."[10] For example, corporations such as TUSincere Holding Group, an industrial and urban development company spun out of Tsinghua University,[11] have capitalized on their access to basic scientific research to build and operate over 300 science parks, which pair academics with technologists in an ecosystem of entrepreneurial resources.[12] A senior executive of TUS Holdings explains that academic tech transfer is key for their business: "Right now in China, it has become very difficult to do a purely real estate business... Real estate companies everywhere are now trying to convert their business from pure real estate to science and technology development. The idea of the science park makes for a good story, which becomes good bargaining power with the government."[13] In addition, TUS emphasizes its ability to bring in high-quality

---

10. Interview with author at MIT Beijing New City Forum, November 2018.
11. TUSincere Holding Group is also an industry member of the MIT China Future City Research Consortium.
12. Interview with author, June 2018.
13. Interview with author, June 2018.

primary, middle, and high schools to their urban developments, again by collaborating with Tsinghua University; this helps them attract talented workers to their "science cities," who then chose to stay and raise their families there over the long term. This turn of events has made private developers far more than real estate or construction experts: as they continue to hire PhDs, partner with elite universities, and invest in their own startups, they are increasingly becoming governments' go-to consultants for ideas on how to take advantage of the latest technologies, firms, and industries in new city projects.

That said, there are also many cases where a local, subnational, or national government launches, finances, and coordinates its own new city without hiring the services of a private planner. In the case of Zhengdong New District in Henan Province (see Chapter 6), for example, the economic development agency of the neighbouring Zhengzhou government directly interfaced with desirable firms and anchor entities to recruit them to its new city.[14] Similarly in the case of Pangyo Techno Valley in South Korea (see Chapter 9), an "expert committee" formed by the provincial government of Gyeounggi-do was responsible for negotiating which IT, bio-tech, and R&D entities would be brought in.[15] Whether a local government hires a private planner to act as the central coordinator ultimately depends on the government's capacity and expertise, as well as the private planner's assessment of whether the project has sound economic prospects. This interaction between public and private planning will continue to be an important determinant of the quality, distribution, and profile of new city projects that will continue to be built in the future.

Planning Decisions and Outcomes

From the perspective of the central coordinator at the very start of planning a new city, its objective is to produce desirable economic development outcomes for both the short term and the long term. It has certain resources it can marshal—land, infrastructure, public and private entities, subsidies—but its constant challenge is figuring out how to best combine and coordinate these resources in order to generate the highest synergies among them. In our conceptual model, the determinants of economic development outcomes ("success") are a function of two major factors: *Market Logic* and *Coordination Mechanisms*.

In fact, many central coordinators of new cities (especially entrepreneurial municipal leaders and private developers) have now accumulated some practical knowledge of

---

14. Interviews with Zhengdong New District government officials, June 2018.
15. Interviews with cluster experts and planners in Gyeounggi-do provincial government, December 2018.

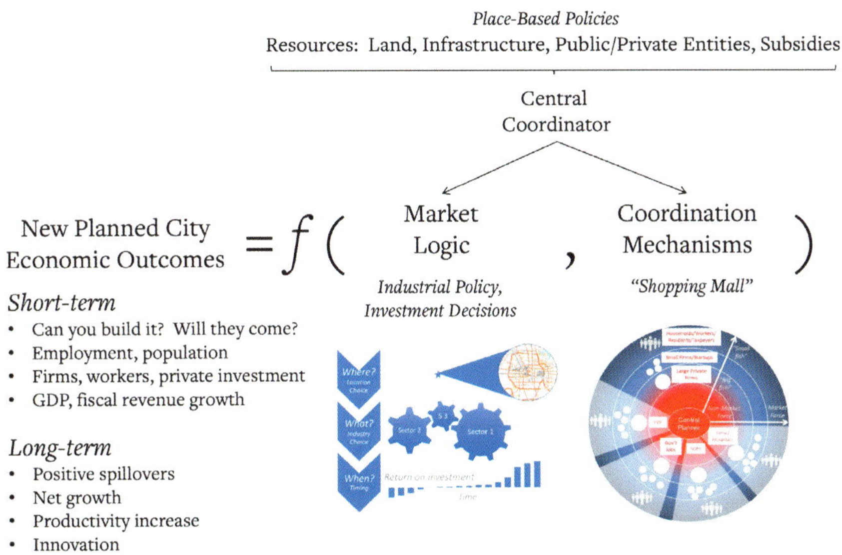

Figure 1.4: Major categories of planning decisions that the central coordinator must make

such mechanisms, and attempt to make decisions based on their own versions of this framework, with the expectation that "systematic and scientific" planning can yield desired outcomes. This, however, is easier said than done, as the rich literature on the historical failures of rational comprehensive planning (for example, in the 1960s US context) cautions. As with any large-scale coordination project in the public realm, it is extremely challenging to mediate political disagreements (e.g. between vertical levels of government or between the government and local residents), to reach across fractured jurisdictions in public policy (e.g. between transportation, land development, environmental protection, and industrial policy), and to transcend limitations in organizational capacity and information to make prescient investment decisions. This is true even in such contexts of strong and centralized state power as China. In addition, the lack (or perhaps impossibility) of a truly "systematic and scientific" procedure for executing such projects, and the deviation of individual decision makers' objective functions from what would be socially optimal, leads to divergences between desired outcomes and real outcomes. In full awareness of these divergences, this conceptual framework is intended not as a recipe, but as a means to elucidate the many dimensions on which coordination must be achieved in order to bring all the parts together, and, correspondingly, the many potential points of conflict and error that are also possible over the course of a new city project.

Market Logic

First, no matter who occupies the role of the central coordinator in a new city project—whether a national government, subnational government, or a private planner—it must make industrial policies and investment decisions that make sense to the market. Beyond the initial "subsidy shock" provided by the central coordinator's first investments—or if the coordinator is a government entity with the power to forcibly relocate public sector entities or SOEs, beyond their initial transplants—the medium to long-term growth of the city depends on its self-sustaining ability to attract further private investment, firms, and workers on its own merits. The central coordinator must therefore adhere to market fundamentals no matter how well-capitalized or politically-connected it is, and seek to invest its bundle of resources at the right place at the right time for the right sector. The central coordinator must make market-driven decisions along three key dimensions: 1. *Where?* 2. *What?* and 3. *When?*

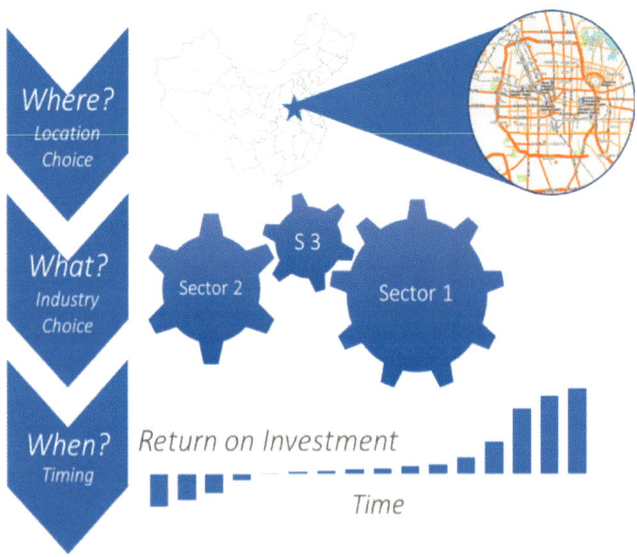

Figure 1.5: "Market Logic" decisions

1. *Where? Location Choice*

First, the site needs to be close enough to a strong existing urban and industrial center to be able to attract firms willing to move their business there (as well as workers and residents willing to live there), but also far enough away to have significantly lower land prices—allowing planners to offer cheap property as an incentive to move out of the big city and to cut the costs of building everything from scratch.[16] The stronger the economic fundamentals of the location, the trickier it is to find large greenfield areas that balance proximity and price.

In addition, being close to the high concentration of existing industrial activity in first- or second-tier cities makes it easier to capture their spillovers when they expand, as residents increasingly seek urban life without the negative externalities associated with large established cities. Prominent new city developers in China, for example, prefer peripheral sites located about 50 to 80 kilometers from one of three established "industrial epicenters": the Beijing-Tianjin belt in the northeast, the Yangtze River Delta on the central coast, and the Pearl River Delta in the south.[17] These three regions cover less than 3% of China's landmass, contribute over a third of the country's GDP, and house almost a fifth of its population (E-House China & Wharton School of Business 2018).

2. *What? Industry Choice*

Once a location has been set (although developers may also work the other way around, and scout out promising locations for a combination of anchor firms they have already committed to "place"), the next most important question becomes what industries should be prioritized in that location. Crucially, this part of the process requires planners to not only create a master plan for every aspect of the city's physical form and land use; it also requires them to explicitly program its economic rationale for existence, cherry-picking the pillar industries of the city well before actual firms, workers, and residents even enter the picture. Planners then customize the physical facilities and business policies of the new city to fulfill the anticipated needs of the chosen industries, and market the specialized expertise of a new place-based economy ("logistics city," "hi-tech," fin-tech city," etc.) before it even exists—essentially betting that if they set good industrial policies, *If you build it, they will come.*

In recent years, explicit strategies of "smart specialization" (Foray, David, and Hall 2009)—or the idea that regions should specialize in sectors that build on

16. Interview by author of an industrial park manager at Fosun Group, in Shanghai, January 2019.
17. Interview by author with a CFLD analyst, in Shanghai, January 2019.

their existing strengths in order to make the most of returns on "scale, scope, and spillovers" (Crespo et al. 2017)—have been adopted in places like the European Union. The million-dollar question still remains: what are the right industries for the right places? In hopes of answering this question for their region, high-capacity governments and private planners are increasingly engaging in systematic research to analyze global, national, and regional industrial trends, mapping the presence of relevant companies throughout the country and province as well as regional factors for innovation and production.[18] Such analyses increasingly use "big data" (such as data from remote sensors, satellites, nighttime lights, cellphone usage, public transportation, flights, transactions, consumption, commuting times, demographic changes) to draw a composite picture of where the "invisible corridor" is in a region of interest, which informs where the new city should be sited.

Still, despite these advances in research, industrial policy remains a politically motivated decision in China's new cities. Developers report that in order to maximize their chances of winning local government approval for a new city project, they tend to make it easy for officials to fulfill their career performance criteria, by suggesting priority sectors that align with the Communist Party's latest national development strategies (such as China's 2025 Intelligent Manufacturing strategy).[19] Despite the fact that countless studies have emphasized the notorious difficulty of replicating successful industrial clusters and innovation hubs like Silicon Valley using deductive, "one-size-fits-all"-minded recipes,[20] developers report that local governments tend to all want the same handful of highly desirable "knowledge economy" sectors—finance, IT, the life sciences, advanced manufacturing, biomedical R&D—regardless of whether they make sense in the context of their region's factor endowment or what their rewalistic comparative advantage might be.[21] This raises risks of misallocation and homogenization (which we will return to at the end of this chapter).

3. *When? Timing Choice*

Even with highly promising location and industry choices in front of them, the central coordinator must weigh the cost of development today (which may be cheap, but more fraught with unknowns about the future of the region) versus development in the future (which may be more informed but also potentially more expensive). Macroeconomic and demographic factors—such as the supply of urban housing relative to population growth and movement—must also be considered decades in

---

18. Presentation by industrial researchers at CFLD Industrial Research Institute in Beijing, January 2019.
19. Interview by author with CFLD analyst in Shanghai, January 2019.
20. For examples, see: Mae Phillips and Wai-chung Yeung (2003), Miao and Hall (2014), and Pfotenhauer and Jasanoff (2017).
21. Interviews by author with large Chinese real estate developers at MIT Beijing New City Forum, November 2018.

advance. The long project timelines of new cities—which can stretch into years, if not decades of vacancy and negative cash flow before seeing residents move in or returns to investment—require the central coordinator to bear significant financial risk. Over the long years of the project, the coordinator must avoid the temptation to sell the land to the highest bidder that comes along (usually looking to build high-margin, luxury real estate) for a one-off fiscal infusion. Instead, the land must be reserved for slow-to-develop clusters and non-revenue generating uses (such as business service centers, public research institutes, parks, or university campuses) that will eventually feed into a greater industrial eco-system. This requires the coordinator to maintain long-term control over the project, even as local and regional politicians pass in and out of office.

Developers and governments report that it usually takes at least five to ten years for the first wave of companies to move into a new city. Until they do, the central coordinators must go without positive cash flow while also investing their largest expenses to lay the groundwork and infrastructural core of the new city. Only once housing begins selling, usually between years five and ten of the project, will they recoup enough revenue to start building out the industrial "engine" of the new city in earnest. Planners and government leaders are also realizing that even with solid fundamentals, it can still take decades for new cities to become fully inhabited, much less fully "vibrant." Zhengdong New District, for example, a new city project in Henan province, was depicted as a "ghost city of new towers with no residents, desolate condos and vacant subdivisions uninhabited for miles and mile and miles" by the US news program *60 Minutes* in 2013, along with similar comments from *Business Insider* and the *Daily Mail*.[22] However, just two years later in 2015, the city was logging a population of over 1.4 million.[23] All of these aspects of a new city's development timeline and life cycle illustrate the central coordinator's challenge, as conditions evolve dynamically over time, rather than remaining static, well-defined trade-offs.

How? Coordination Mechanisms

Upon making the industrial policies and major investment decisions of *Where*, *What*, and *When*—which underpin the Market Logic of the new city—the central coordinator must then act as the owner of their metaphorical "shopping mall," and begin coordinating the movements of the public and private entities they want to seed their new city. Their constant challenge is the question, *If we build it, will they come?*

---

22. Qtd. in Wade Shepard (2015)
23. Interviews with Zhengdong New District officials, June 2018.

There appear to be three prominent pathways through which the central coordinator tries to compel firms, workers, investors, and residents to come:

1) A subnational government (or in some cases, the national government, as in Xiong'an New Area in Hebei, China) acts as the central coordinator, and directly reaches out to firms in the market. This usually works best if there is already strong market demand to move into the city regardless of the coordinator's abilities, such that the government does not need to actively pursue firms in the market through personal or professional relationships (for an example, see Chapter 5).

2) A subnational government acts as the central coordinator and uses state control to forcibly move public and semi-public entities into its city. This usually works best if the government body has considerable political power as was the case in Zhengdong New District, China, where the government managed to move the headquarters of the provincial government of Henan, a provincial-level industrial park, and several top universities (see Chapter 6).

3) A private developer acts as the central coordinator on behalf of a weak local government and interfaces with private firms in the market. This usually works best if the developer has a large network of corporate contacts (for example, if it is

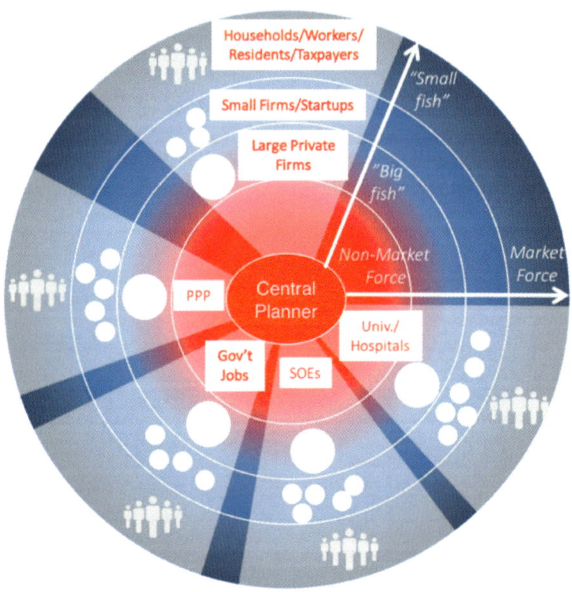

Figure 1.6: The central coordinator at the center uses both non-market (political) and market mechanisms to attract both non-market entities (e.g. universities, hospitals, SOEs, government jobs) and market entities (private firms, workers).

the real estate branch of a larger state-owned enterprise or conglomerate, such as China Resources Land, which is part of China Resources Group), or if it has specific experience building specialized types of new planned cities (such as TUSincere, with its special relationship to Tsinghua University). For an example of how such an arrangement works in practice—including how risk is shared, profits are managed, and decisions are made—see the case of Gu'an New Industry City, a project led by the private developer CFLD (Chapter 7).

When we look at the relationships among the different variables in this framework—resources, market logic, and coordination mechanisms—a natural question is, what is each variable's relative value-added to any given new city project? We might imagine that having control over resources (land, subsidies, infrastructure, capital) is a constant that is always required to physically build out a new city, no matter where. But on top of this requisite base, the convergence of strong market logic (good location choice, industrial policy, and timing) with strong coordination mechanisms (recruitment of big and small fish, and the creation of a new industrial agglomeration) would provide the most fertile conditions for an economically successful new city. On the other end of the spectrum, a combination of weak resources, weak market logic, and weak coordination mechanisms lends itself to a "ghost city" scenario, a new city project with physical structures but little or no economic or human vibrancy. The mid-spectrum scenarios—where most new city projects likely fall—are less clear: what outcomes could be expected in a scenario with strong market logic but weak coordination, or weak market logic but strong coordination capacity? Are these two variables substitutes—where strength in one can compensate for weakness in the other—or complements, which only create value in conjunction with the other?

This question has implications for the geography of new cities: if we were to learn that the most value came from the coordination efforts of a good central coordinator—i.e. skills and strategies that can be researched, trained, improved, and hired—rather than from the market fundamentals of its location, this would greatly expand the range of places where new cities could be built and expected to flourish. If, however, we were to learn that the value created from coordination provides only a small premium on top of the bulk of the value that comes from strong fundamentals—i.e. if it really is *location, location, location* that matters for the economic vibrancy of new cities—then it would greatly constrain the range of possible sites. Our current hypothesis is that these two factors are both supplements and complements, and the relative magnitudes might vary across different locations and contexts. For instance, they strengthen each other (complementarity) when both market fundamentals and coordination capacity are strong, whereas if one factor is relatively weak, the other can, to some extent, bring in extra strength and new value to make up for the original disadvantages. These speculations call for more case studies and systematic analysis, by which a spectrum of new city outcomes across geographies might be compared.

New Opportunities, New Risks

On the upside, we have argued that new cities planned as new economic engines have the potential to create positive-sum value. A central coordinator can theoretically resolve state and market failures—solving problems of large-scale land assembly, place-based resource bundling, first mover reluctance, and cross-firm coordination—to encourage complementary firms to cluster together in a timely fashion, and cultivate a holistic and vibrant urban environment where people can reside for life. If the central coordinator successfully accomplishes these sophisticated tasks, firms and workers can capture positive externalities from agglomeration and become more productive than the sum of their parts. In this way, a new city founded on the basis of thoughtfully derived, market-driven industrial policy may allow the region to develop in directions that are considered desirable for long-term growth, rather than in an uncontrolled, speculative manner (for example, avoiding a proliferation of high-end, residential development only for the wealthiest buyers).

In addition, the increased involvement of private actors in the planning process may present an opportunity for the market to correct state-led over-investment in unsound new city projects. Strong political incentives pushing local governments to raise land-based municipal financing—as well as low construction costs, state-owned urban land, and central stimulation after the 2008 financial crisis—led to a breakout of "new city fever" in China between 2009 and 2012 (Lu 2011), where the majority of projects were built in inland regions with low density, large distances to existing urban centers, and large population outflows (Chang and Lu 2017). Many are now at risk of turning into ghost towns due to insufficient demand for jobs or housing in these areas (Batty 2016). One quantification of this gap finds that residential districts of new cities are only about 8.8% as "vibrant" as those in older urban areas (Jin et al. 2017).

Because private planners operate under different parameters than local governments and are bound by different constraints, they may help increase the quality, rather than the quantity of new city projects. For example, whereas local governments have a fixed spatial jurisdiction, developers are footloose, which allows them to selectively launch projects at the strongest sites. Local governments often only have enough land and resources to attempt to build a new city once in their respective regions, whereas successful developers can run multiple projects in multiple regions, allowing them to learn from their mistakes. And while government officials may eventually face negative political consequences if their new city project fails to produce long-term returns on investment, market-driven private developers literally go out of business if that occurs.

But having addressed the upsides of this model of new city making, we must also raise the potential for significant and novel downsides. For one, there is the risk of private and public incompetence in planning. Private planners may still make poor investment decisions and create white elephant projects that cost enormous sums to build but fail to ever create value. Ongoing debates on the "how to" of implementing good, top-down interventions—whether industrial policies should follow comparative advantage or leap vertically or laterally in industrial space (Lin and Chang 2009); whether regions should specialize or diversify (Kemeny and Storper 2015); or how to identify a region's best bets for "smart specialization" in the first place—highlight the challenges policy-makers face when trying to operationalize these ideas in practice. What new risks arise when, as economist Albert Saiz puts it, "real estate developers need to become macroeconomists" (Saiz 2018)?

Another risk is that political incentives may still drive planning decisions and continue to cause misallocation errors and even oversupply of such new cities, particularly through local industrial policy. Prominent Chinese developers recount that government officials frequently disagree with their recommendations on which sectors to prioritize in their region, because they optimize for political prestige rather than comparative advantage.[24] Many note that "governments will not accept answers they don't want to hear, sometimes, about what sectors make sense in their city," and only want to consider "high-end" sectors regardless of fit, even though "there are only a few 'top' sectors and a few 'big fish' within those sectors."[25] Others complain that "all local governments, no matter whether they are first-tier or fourth-tier, want to have a financial hub in their new city, or a 'cloud-based big data hub'—even though these need a lot of water to generate enough electricity, like in Guizhou province. They need to think of their match with natural resources!"[26]

Relatedly, scholars have noted that many new planned cities, particularly in Asia and especially in China, engage in practices of modeling, emulating, and "inter-referencing" other cities that are perceived as globally successful or "world-class," which has led to the spread of highly homogenous new city projects across many regional contexts (Roy and Ong 2011). Scholars have primarily criticized these inter-referential and emulative practices on aesthetic, sociological, and cultural grounds, arguing that they perpetuate certain homogenous visions and performances of urbanity, modernity, and success, while rejecting local, indigenous, or alternative visions, intelligences, and practices.

To these perspectives, we add that homogenization of industrial specialization also poses potential risk from a macroeconomic perspective. Homogeneity, over-concentration, and copying was already a problem for existing cities in China.

24. Interview by author with industrial researchers at CFLD Industrial Research Institute in Beijing, January 2019.
25. Interviews by author at MIT Beijing New City Forum, November 2018.
26. Ibid.

Geographer Fulong Wu finds that "most cities in the YRD [Yangtze River Delta] aimed to develop export-oriented industries, based on the successful development of Suzhou and Wuxi. Eight out of 16 cities in the YRD selected petrochemical industries, 11 selected automobile parts manufacturing, and 12 selected IT and communication equipment. Almost all cities along the Yangtze River, coastal Jiangsu, and Hangzhou Bay proposed to develop similar export-oriented industries and thus competed for raw materials in the same market" (Wu 2016). Wu notes that in the absence of diversification, competing cities race to the bottom in the same markets, which leads to lower profit margins, environmental degradation, excessive rural-to-urban conversion, and the fragmentation of regional governance.

If all new cities continue to prioritize the same handful of desirable, high-skill, "knowledge economy" sectors—IT, finance, life sciences, e-commerce—regardless of their respective fit, they may be at risk of following the same trend and over-competing with each other over finite resources in sectors it never made sense for them to specialize in the first place. If 11 out of 16 cities in the Yangtze River Delta have already chosen to specialize in auto parts manufacturing, and some high proportion of "new industry" cities are planned to specialize in autonomous vehicle manufacturing, not all of them will end up like Leipzeig, Germany—far more of them are likely to become like Detroit, Michigan in the not-too-distant future.

Last, there are large outstanding unknowns about many aspects of new cities as economic engines. Importantly, for any given project it is difficult to know whether the creation of the new city was responsible for an expansion of economic activities on net, or whether those same firms would have been just as or even more productive in other places—in other words, did building the new city expand the pie, or simply reshuffle market and non-market resources from other places? Though we assume that market actors freely choose to relocate to new cities based on their own individual cost-benefit analyses, there has not been a study of their realized benefits from agglomeration and the changes in long-term productivity over time. This is one of many empirical and theoretical questions that researchers will need to approach in the future, as new cities mature.

Another natural question is, where else in the world would this kind of intensive coordination capacity be possible? Can we expect to see new planned cities in the advanced industrial democracies of the world, or is this an experiment only the Chinese Communist Party could possibly run? On the demand side of this question, it must be remembered that China still expects significant rural-to-urban migration over the next few decades, whereas many other developing and developed countries seem to have reached an equilibrium. Migrants seeking better opportunities flow into existing megacities, many of which are already overburdened with heavy congestion and pollution, inadequate housing infrastructure, and low governance capacity. These problems are being experienced and dealt with in many different places in many different ways, one of which is to build more cities. On the supply side, new cities are extremely difficult to construct in countries where there is little large-scale land available for development that is neither privately owned nor protected for public usage (e.g. national park reserves). It would thus be surprising to see new cities emerge in the US or western Europe; the equivalent "economic engines" in these countries are being developed through urban renewal or through creating "innovation districts" in existing cities through similar processes of industrial recruitment and agglomeration. As the other case studies in the rest of this book and in the urban studies literature demonstrate, new cities are being created through centralized coordination in a range of countries with different political economic regimes than China—including India (Chapter 9), Malaysia (Chapter 8), and South Korea (Chapter 9)—but often with far greater difficulties in both land assembly and political will. Thus from both a demand- and supply-side perspective, China is an exceptional political economy in many ways, and its successes and failures must be studied as such: not necessarily as prescriptions or templates for other places in the world to build new cities just like its new cities, but as a critical case of urbanization in its own right, which offers insights for other places and practitioners.

There are other critical problems that we have not addressed in this brief introductory chapter: normative questions of governance and public accountability; the ethics of social displacement, equity, and access; the environmental impact of greenfield construction; and the lived experience of residing in a new city as an urban environment, to name just a few. These are critical issues that have occupied many urban scholars on this subject—and for good reason. Through our focus on the economic development potential of new cities as new economic engines, we hope to contribute another angle to the study of this important phenomenon, and throw light on the many questions we have about the world of new cities being built at rapid scale, scope, and spread today.

References

Alder, Simon, Lin Shao, and Fabrizio Zilibotti. 2016. "Economic Reforms and Industrial Policy in a Panel of Chinese Cities." *Journal of Economic Growth* 21 (4): 305–349.

Al-Filali, Isam Yahia, and Giulio M. Gallarotti. 2012. "Smart Development: Saudi Arabia's Quest for a Knowledge Economy." *International Studies* 49 (1–2): 47–76.

Batty, Michael. 2016. "Empty Buildings, Shrinking Cities and Ghost Towns." *Environment and Planning B: Planning and Design* 43 (1): 3–6.

Bunnell, Tim, Michelle Ann Miller, Nicholas A. Phelps, and John Taylor. 2013. "Urban Development in a Decentralized Indonesia: Two Success Stories?" *Pacific Affairs* 86 (4): 857–876.

Chang, Chen, and Ming Lu. 2017. "Misery of New Town——Density, Distance and Debt." *China Economic Quarterly* no. 4: 16.

Crespo, J., P. A. Balland, R. Boschma, and D. Rigby. 2017. "Regional Diversification Opportunities and Smart Specialization Strategies." *Publications Office of the European Union.*

Datta, Ayona. 2015. "New Urban Utopias of Postcolonial India: 'Entrepreneurial Urbanization'in Dholera Smart City, Gujarat." *Dialogues in Human Geography* 5 (1): 3–22.

Datta, Ayona, and Abdul Shaban. 2016. *Mega-Urbanization in the Global South: Fast Cities and New Urban Utopias of the Postcolonial State.* Routledge.

Dieleman, Marleen. 2011. "New Town Development in Indonesia: Renegotiating, Shaping and Replacing Institutions." *Bijdragen Tot de Taal-, Land-En Volkenkunde/ Journal of the Humanities and Social Sciences of Southeast Asia* 167 (1): 60–85.

Douglass, Mike, and Liling Huang. 2007. "Globalizing the City in Southeast Asia: Utopia on the Urban Edge–the Case of Phu My Hung, Saigon." *International Journal of Asia Pacific Studies* 3 (2): 1–42.

Duranton, Gilles, and Anthony J. Venables. 2018. *Place-Based Policies for Development.* The World Bank.

E-House China & Wharton School of Business. 2018. "CFLD's Gu'an New Industry City: A New Kind of Public-Private Partnership." Knowledge@Wharton. March 2, 2018. https://knowledge.wharton.upenn.edu/article/cflds-guan-new-industry-city-new-kind-public-private-partnership/.

Foray, Dominique, Paul A. David, and Bronwyn Hall. 2009. "Smart Specialisation–the Concept." *Knowledge Economists Policy Brief* 9 (85): 100.

Glaeser, Edward L., and Joshua D. Gottlieb. 2008. "The Economics of Place-Making Policies." National Bureau of Economic Research. NBER Working Paper No. 14373.

Gould, Eric D., B. Peter Pashigian, and Canice J. Prendergast. 2005. "Contracts, Externalities, and Incentives in Shopping Malls." *Review of Economics and Statistics* 87 (3): 411–422.

Herbert, Claire W., and Martin J. Murray. 2015. "Building from Scratch: New Cities, Privatized Urbanism and the Spatial Restructuring of Johannesburg after Apartheid." *International Journal of Urban and Regional Research* 39 (3): 471–494.

Jin, Xiaobin, Ying Long, Wei Sun, Yuying Lu, Xuhong Yang, and Jingxian Tang. 2017. "Evaluating Cities' Vitality and Identifying Ghost Cities in China with Emerging Geographical Data." *Cities* 63: 98–109.

Jo, Heeyoung Angie. 2019. "Coordination vs. control: planning new cities as new economic engines in China." MCP diss., Massachusetts Institute of Technology, 2019.

Kahn, Matthew E., Weizeng Sun, Jianfeng Wu, and Siqi Zheng. 2018. "The Revealed Preference of the Chinese Communist Party Leadership: Investing in Local Economic Development versus Rewarding Social Connections." National Bureau of Economic Research. NBER Working Paper No. 24457.

Keeton, Rachel. 2011. *Rising in the East: Contemporary New Towns in Asia.* International New Town Institute, Amsterdam: SUN Architecture

Kemeny, Thomas, and Michael Storper. 2015. "Is Specialization Good for Regional Economic Development?" *Regional Studies* 49 (6): 1003–1018.

Lin, Justin, and Ha-Joon Chang. 2009. "Should Industrial Policy in Developing Countries Conform to Comparative Advantage or Defy It? A Debate between Justin Lin and Ha-Joon Chang." *Development Policy Review* 27 (5): 483–502.

Lu, Ming. 2011. "The Interregional Reallocation of Construction Land Use Right: A New Impetus of Chinese Economic Growth." *The Journal of World Economy* 1: 107–125.

Mae Phillips, Su-Ann, and Henry Wai-chung Yeung. 2003. "A Place for R&D? The Singapore Science Park." *Urban Studies* 40 (4): 707–732.

Miao, Julie Tian, and Peter Hall. 2014. "Optical Illusion? The Growth and Development of the Optics Valley of China." *Environment and Planning C: Government and Policy* 32 (5): 863–879.

Moser, Sarah. 2015. "New Cities: Old Wine in New Bottles?" *Dialogues in Human Geography* 5 (1): 31–35.

Moser, Sarah, Marian Swain, and Mohammed H. Alkhabbaz. 2015. "King Abdullah Economic City: Engineering Saudi Arabia's Post-Oil Future." *Cities* 45: 71–80.

Neumark, David, and Helen Simpson. 2015. "Place-Based Policies." In *Handbook of Regional and Urban Economics*, 5:1197–1287. Elsevier.

Pashigian, B. Peter, and Eric D. Gould. 1998. "Internalizing Externalities: The Pricing of Space in Shopping Malls." *The Journal of Law and Economics* 41 (1): 115–142.

Percival, Tom, and Paul Waley. 2012. "Articulating Intra-Asian Urbanism: The Production of Satellite Cities in Phnom Penh." *Urban Studies* 49 (13): 2873–2888.

Pfotenhauer, Sebastian, and Sheila Jasanoff. 2017. "Panacea or Diagnosis? Imaginaries of Innovation and the 'MIT Model'in Three Political Cultures." *Social Studies of Science* 47 (6): 783–810.

Rizzo, Agatino. 2017. "Why Knowledge Megaprojects Will Fail to Transform Gulf Countries in Post-Carbon Economies: The Case of Qatar." *Journal of Urban Technology* 24 (3): 85–98.

Rizzo, Agatino, and John Glasson. 2012. "Iskandar Malaysia." *Cities* 29 (6): 417–427.

Roy, Ananya, and Aihwa Ong. 2011. "Introduction." In *Worlding Cities: Asian Experiments and the Art of Being Global*. Vol. 42. John Wiley & Sons.

Saiz, Albert. 2018. "International Housing Economics & Finance." Lecture presented at the MIT Department of Urban Studies and Planning, February 20.

Shatkin, Gavin. 2011. "Planning Privatopolis: Representation and Contestation in the Development of Urban Integrated Mega-Projects." *Worlding Cities: Asian Experiments and the Art of Being Global*, 77–97.

Shepard, Wade. 2015. "Banishing the Ghost." South China Morning Post. May 26, 2015. https://www.scmp.com/presented/topics/go-china-zhengzhou/article/1802853/banishing-ghost.

Shepard, Wade. 2017. "Why Hundreds Of Completely New Cities Are Being Built Around The World." Forbes. December 12, 2017. https://www.forbes.com/sites/wadeshepard/2017/12/12/why-hundreds-of-completely-new-cities-are-being-built-around-the-world/.

Shepard, Wade. 2018. "How The Growth Of New Cities Is Becoming A Global Economic Driver." Forbes. May 31, 2018. https://www.forbes.com/sites/wadeshepard/2018/05/31/how-the-growth-of-new-cities-is-becoming-a-global-economic-driver/.

Tok, Evren, Jason James McSparren, Maha Al Merekhi, Hanaa Elghaish, and Fatema Mohamed Ali. 2015. "Crafting Smart Cities in the Gulf Region: A Comparison of Masdar and Lusail." In *Handbook of Research on Digital Media and Creative Technologies*, 448–460. IGI Global.

Van Noorloos, Femke, and Marjan Kloosterboer. 2018. "Africa's New Cities: The Contested Future of Urbanisation." *Urban Studies* 55 (6): 1223–1241.

Watson, Vanessa. 2014. "African Urban Fantasies: Dreams or Nightmares?" *Environment and Urbanization* 26 (1): 215–231.

Wu, Fulong. 2016. "China's Emergent City-Region Governance: A New Form of State Spatial Selectivity through State-Orchestrated Rescaling." *International Journal of Urban and Regional Research* 40 (6): 1134–1151.

Yin, Guanwen, Yungang Liu, and Fenglong Wang. 2018. "Emerging Chinese New Towns: Local Government-Directed Capital Switching in Inland China." *Cities* 79: 102–112.

Zhang, Qiming, Ying Zeng, Jinsong Deng, Ke Wang, Ruowei Jiang, and Ziran Ye. 2017. "'Ghost Cities' Identification Using Multi-Source Remote Sensing Datasets: A Case Study in Yangtze River Delta." *Applied Geography* 80:112-121.

Zheng, Siqi, Weizeng Sun, Jianfeng Wu, and Matthew E. Kahn. 2017. "The Birth of Edge Cities in China: Measuring the Effects of Industrial Parks Policy." *Journal of Urban Economics* 100: 80–103.

Chapter 2.

Vibrant Cities or Ghost Towns? Measurement of Urban Vibrancy and its Application in China

Jianfeng Wu, Yicheng Zhao[1]

Introduction

The rapid shift of population from rural to urban has changed the economic landscape of Asian countries. One of the prominent urbanization trends in Asia is the emergence of hundreds of new planned cities built by city governments. These new cities are developed with modern design and futuristic architecture near the inner cities on hitherto unused or underused areas. As local governments in this region have ambitions to move toward urban-based economies, these cities are expected to accommodate high-tech, research, and development (R&D) centers, modern shopping malls, new transportation hubs, industrial zones, and large-scale housing in gated communities for middle class residents. Planning for the growth of these cites would be challenging for any local government in this region. Critics of new planned cities argue that the cost of building them is too high and the supply of new cities may outgrow the demand for them, leading to a serious oversupply problem and wasteful investment. Such "ghost towns" are located in several parts of Asia. On the other hand, some new planned cities are inhabited as they create jobs and promote industrial growth.

This chapter will consider several new planned cities in China, and its goal is to provide a simple way to measure the urban economic vibrancy of these new planned cities using data over the past several years. It particularly explores whether new built cities have been successful in accommodating a high population density and economic activities, and then try to explain the driving forces behind urban economic vibrancy.

Background

China is without doubt one of several epicenters of new city development in Asia, having established hundreds of new cities throughout the country over recent decades. New planned cities in China are born of industrial restructuring, with the support of city governments who are attempting to maintain high growth and to shift to urban-based economies. The fast urbanization process since the end of 1980s has led a big number of Chinese cities to move into industrialized economies, despite the fact that such industrialization trends are diverse and uneven. These cities have progressively developed their product sectors in two stages. They initially centered on participating in international trade and being involved in the global division of labor by attracting foreign direct investment (FDI). Then they attempted to create

1. We thank Yinglin Feng and Xueyue Liu from Fudan University and Binli Han from Tongji University for providing excellent research assistance. Jianfeng Wu thanks the National Natural Science Foundation of China (No. 71573054) and financial support from Fudan University Shanghai-Hongkong Development Institute (SHKDI) and Shanghai Institute of International Finance and Economics.

local industrial clustering by exploiting agglomeration economies. As more and more firms from both domestic and foreign markets flowed into these cities, economies of scale, whether in the production of intermediate goods or differentiated products, as well as agglomeration effects within and across industries, generated huge benefits, thus promoting urban growth.

A prime example is Dongguan, China, which has become a "factory of the world"—a city of more than 7 million people that grew from a collection of sleepy villages in China's Pearl River delta (Coulibaly et al. 2008). At the beginning of the 1980s global industrial clusters of labor-intensive goods emerged at Dongguan as they enjoyed the knowledge spillover from FDI and lower logistics costs owing to their proximity to input providers and export traders. As a stronger self-agglomeration took place in the mid-1990s, clusters of telecommunications, electronics, and computer components have dominated Dongguan's industrial landscape.

Currently city governments in China are striving to restructure their economies to move them into urban-based sectors. On one hand, accelerated industrialization allows these cities to amass the necessary wealth and skills to embark upon restructuring programs. On the other hand, these cities face looming labor automation and job displacement in traditional manufacturing sectors such as factory work. In addition, the rapid productivity growth in agriculture-intensive sectors has released millions of new laborers into the urban sector, amplifying the pressure for cities to adapt to technological change. Motivated by these forces, these city governments have been ambitious to develop urban-based economies by expanding growth in high-value industries such as firms related to information and computer technology (ICT) as well as expediting the development of producer services and high-end urban service sectors. The cities need to generate a range of new spaces, including spaces of production, exchange, innovation, and consumption, in order to accommodate these new sectors. In China the process of building new cities at huge scales on the outskirts of core urban areas has been happening since the early 2000s: either the city government plans and constructs a totally new city (or district) by transforming collectively owned land in rural areas into state land; or an adjacent county with a strong, industrial base is incorporated into the urban core area by giving it urban status.[2] For city governments in China, the new cities are not just construction pursuits; they are the new economic engines to create and sustain local growth.

Building and operating a new city is a long-term gamble. Not every new city will

2. In China, a municipality or a prefecture-level city always have several subdivisions, including districts or counties. Districts are mostly urban and suburban in nature, containing mostly urban, built-up areas with little farmland. Counties are the areas with a large towns and townships under them governing rural areas.

evolve into the vibrant place it was originally envisioned to be. Some new cities end up becoming "ghost cities" because they failed to survive. A study by Chinese search giant Baidu identified 50 such dormant, newly built cities in China with vast, uninhabited real estate projects (Chi et al. 2015). Wade Shephard (2015) focused on China's infrastructure boom and provided a comprehensive analysis of the hundreds of empty, new-city projects in various regions in China during its fast-paced urbanization period of 2000s. But Karen Lai (2012) documented another story of China's new city building, the case of Lujiazui Financial City (LFC). LFC has been one of Asia's key financial centers since the beginning of 1990s. It is home to more than 750 licensed financial institutions, more than 12 factor markets for securities, futures, diamond, oil, and financial futures, and 200, 000 of Shanghai's financial professionals. Motivated by the cases in these studies, this chapter attempts to provide a comprehensive assessment on the performance of new planned cities in China over the past decades.

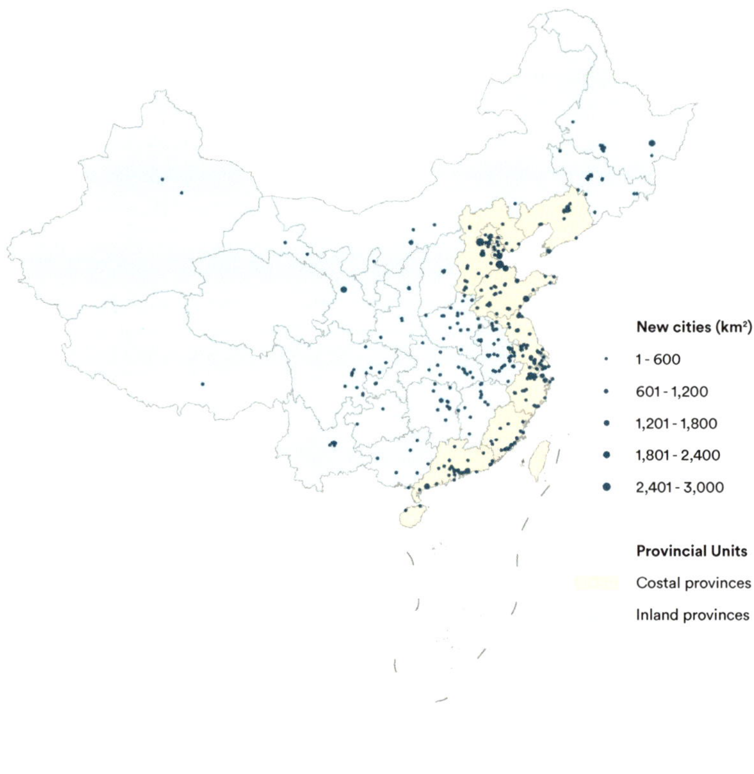

Figure 2.1: The geography of new planned cities across China (in our sample), 1991-2006

New Planned City Sample

To conduct our empirical exercise in this chapter, we manually collected information about 376 new planned cities with exact geography boundaries in China over the period of 1991-2016.[3] This data set was constructed by exploiting the online information online at these new planned cities' websites, which can be searched using Baidu, the first and largest Chinese search engine, using "new city" (Xincheng) and "new district" (Xinqu) as keywords. From this data set we were able to know each new planned city's location, geographic boundary, the year the city was planned, the planned area, the planned population, the planned functions, the government offices, educational and medical facilities, and its big shopping malls. We geocoded these new planned cities (and districts) using the exact boundary information of GIS maps for each prefecture-level-and-above city.

Figure 2.1 illustrates the geographical distribution of these new planned cities across China. Among this new city sample, 57.3 percent of them are located in the coast provinces. If they are grouped according to the host urban areas of different sizes, more than 28.4 percent are concentrated in first and second-tier cities (See classification in OECD (OECD 2015)).

Our data provides evidence that these newly built cities help their hosts shift to urban-based economies. We map the geocoded firms into different new cities and then identify the group of economic activities that a newly built city has attracted. We obtain these firm-level data from the registered-companies dataset annually released by State Administration for Industry and Commerce of China. It provides the following information about companies: name, legal person, registered address, registered capital, registered date, and business scopes. We use such data from 2009 to 2016. Based on the business scope information we keep the companies related to urban-based economies and classify them into three groups: producer service, high-end manufacturing, and high-end service activities. As shown in Figurc 2.2, on average, the newly-built-city shares of these three types of economic activities in their respective host cities are experiencing rising trends: the share of producer-service activities in new cities increases from 15.2% in 2009 to 22.5% in 2006, and the shares of high-end manufacturing and services go up from 17.6% and 15.9% in 2009 to 28.5% and 24.7% in 2016, respectively.

3. In China, it is reported there have been more than 1,000 new planned cities or new cities in constructions since 1990s. In our analysis, we only consider these cities with detailed information especially including exact geography boundary found from their official websites.

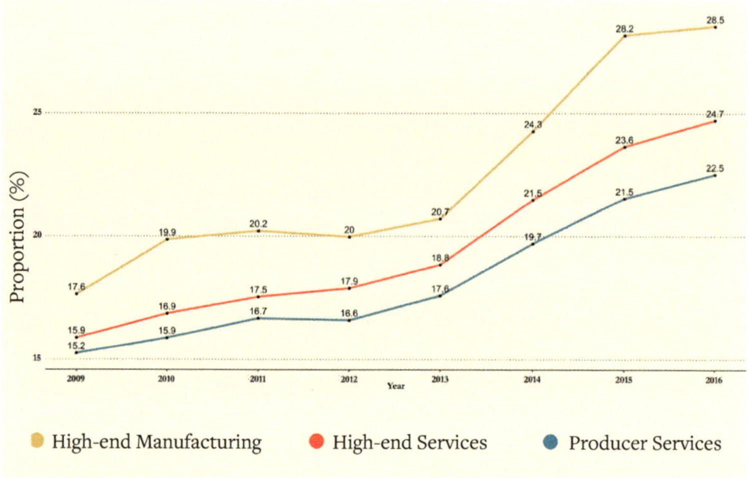

Figure 2.2: The changes in the shares of urban-based economic activities in new planned cities (in our sample), 2009-2016.

Three Ways to Measure New Planned Cities' Economic Vibrancy

In this section, we focus on urban vibrancy, which is defined as the concentration of production and consumption activities as well as the consequent agglomeration economies. We argue that whether a new planned city becomes an economically vibrant area or not depends on its capacity to accommodate a high density of human and business activities.

Measurement

We consider three basic elements to describe the full range of a new planned city, including: (1) the built-up area ratio; (2) the density of the population; and (3) the density of economic activities. The "convergence" of these three urban elements is assumed to reflect the degree of economic vibrancy. For example, a city with high ratio of built-up area but lower density population and economic activities is featured as less vibrant. In our analysis, the built-up area ratio (BR) is calculated as the ratio of built-up pixels to all the pixels within the exact boundary of a new city. The population density is measured thousands of persons per unit of land. The density of economic activities (ED) is captured by the standard information on light radiance measured by satellite at night. Nighttime light radiance has been widely used as a proxy for economic activity at the finer, spatial level.

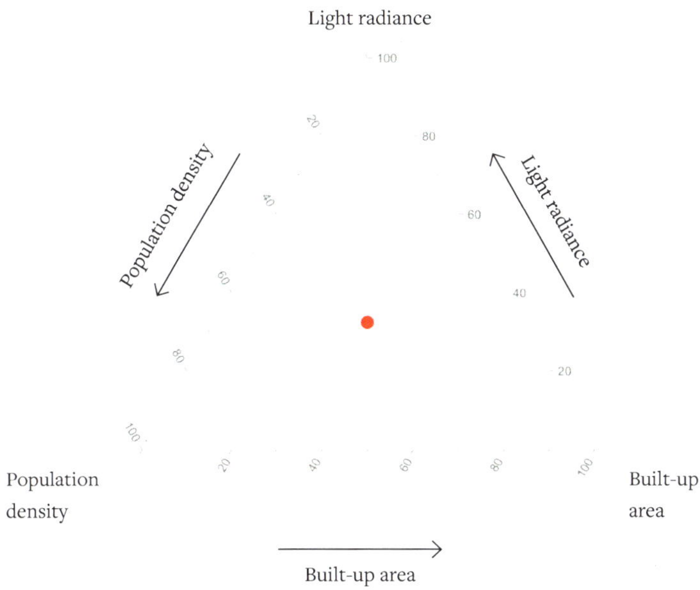

Figure 2.3: Illustration of a ternary diagram representing the development stages of a planned city

To measure such convergence we employ a ternary contour approach that originated in earth science to demonstrate the classification of soil textures and was then widely applied in other fields including geography.[4] In our analysis, the ternary diagram (Figure 2.3) consists of three axes at 60 degree angles to each other, and the three corners of the triangle represent the composition of a new planned city—built-up area, population density, and density of economic activities (measured as light radiance) each of which add up to a constant (100%). Points within the triangle represent ternary mixtures of these three components. The side opposite to a corner is defined as a pure component (built-up area, population density, or light radiance). Nonetheless the ternary diagram usefully represents the evolution process of a new planned city. The central point (red point) in the triangle has equal levels of built-up area, density of population, and density of economic activities, representing a highest degree of convergence. A city plotted by this point indicates that its built-up area has been fully occupied by people and economic activities. A point away from the central point is an unbalanced composition—as for example a city represented

4. One of the disadvantages of this contour method is that there lacks economic sense for some extreme points in the graph. For example, a city with 100% level of population density but with zero level of built-up ratio and luminosity, or a city with 100% level of luminosity with zero level of built-up ratio and population density, would not be necessitated by any physical or economic principle.

by a point in the region left to the central point but toward the built-up area.[5]

Following Zhang et al. (2017), the sum of these three components is constructed be 100% as follows:

$$P_{BR} = \frac{RANK_{BR}}{RANK_{BR} + RANK_{PD} + RANK_{ED}}$$
$$P_{PD} = \frac{RANK_{PD}}{RANK_{BR} + RANK_{PD} + RANK_{ED}}$$
$$P_{ED} = \frac{RANK_{ED}}{RANK_{BR} + RANK_{PD} + RANK_{ED}}$$

where P_{BR}, P_{PD}, and P_{ED} are the relative percentages of built-up area, population density, and density of economic activities, respectively. $RANK_{BR}$ represents each city's rank in terms of the magnitude of built-up area in an ascending order. Similarly, $RANK_{PD}$ and $RANK_{ED}$ are the ranks for each city in ascending order with respect to its population density and the density of economic activities, respectively. Using the three corresponding coordinate values, we are able to plot the location of each new city (district) in the ternary contour.

For a new planned city, the *urban vibrancy* is calculated as the Euclidean distance (in absolute value) between its location in the ternary contour and the central point of this contour. The shorter the distance, the more vibrant a new planned city is or the higher its urban vibrancy is.

Data

We rely on a variety of data sources to measure the three components of a new planned city:

- The *built-up area* information is from Land Cover Type Remoting Sensing Image Data in China provided by the Resource and Environment Data Cloud Platform. This platform releases five-year, shape files for 1X1 km^2 grids of land areas covering China across different types of land uses including forest, agriculture, grassroots, water, built up land, and unutilized land. We use the 2015 data released in 2017.

5. Among the points within the triangle, some are closer to the corner of light radiance. This means cities contains high level of light radiance but with low levels of built-up and population density. Such a composition may indicate the ongoing construction of these newly cities. Those proximate to the corner of population density indicate another set of cases, in which the villages in rural areas have been transferred to urban land use but the rural people have not moved out.

- The *population density* at the grid level is calculated using a spatial allocation model of population provided by Resource and Environment Data Cloud Platform (REDCP). In this model, the 1x1 km^2 grids of population are calculated by distributing the aggregated, county-level population into different grids weighted by grid-level land type, nighttime light density, and residential zone density. In this chapter, we consider the 2015 Population Grid of China released on this REDCP platform.

- The *density of economic activities* is captured by the standard information on light radiance measured by satellite at night. We use the 2016 nightlight data from the National Centers for Environmental Information at the National Oceanic and Atmospheric Administration (NCEI-NOOA). Following Matt Lowe's cleaning procedure (Lowe 2014), we aggregate the data into grid cells of size 0.25X0.25 degrees.

Figure 2.4 (a)-(c) illustrate the location of Zhengdong New City, one of our new city examples, with nighttime light radiance, built-up area, and population density, respectively.

Illustrations of Urban Vibrancy across New Planned Cities

We locate the new city sample we have collected in the ternary contour with three coordinated values related to urban vibrancy. The samples located directly on the left and right lines of the triangle are dropped since their constructions, although planned, have not begun. As depicted in Figure 2.5, we find that a larger share of points is located around the center of the diagram, implying that quite a number of new cities in our sample have a tendency to move toward the central point (highlighted in red) with similar levels of the three components, built-up area, light radiance, and population density. Moreover, the color-shaded polygon enclosing areas of the triad with successively higher likelihood of containing new city points are found to be near the corner of built-up area. This suggests that the less vibrant new cities are characterized as massive built-up areas with a low density of population or low density of economic activities.

We examine the geographic variations in urban vibrancy using similar ternary contour approach when new cities are classified into two groups: those on the coast and those in the interior. It is found that new planned cities on the coast perform better than those in the interior in terms of the convergence of the three components of urban vibrancy—coastal new cities enjoy greater urban vibrancy. We also investigate whether the urban vibrancy varies across cities of different sizes, and we find that that the new planned cities in big metropolitan areas tend to achieve greater urban vibrancy than those not in big metropolitan areas.

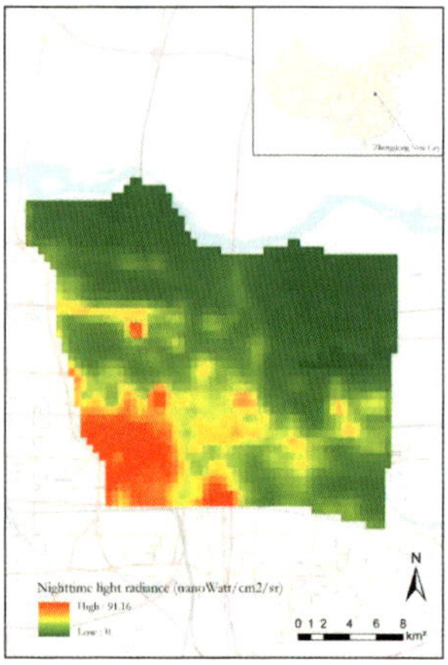

Nighttime light radiance (nanoWatt/cm2/sr)

High: 91.16

Low: 0

Figure 2.4 (b): Location of Zhengdong New City with built-up area

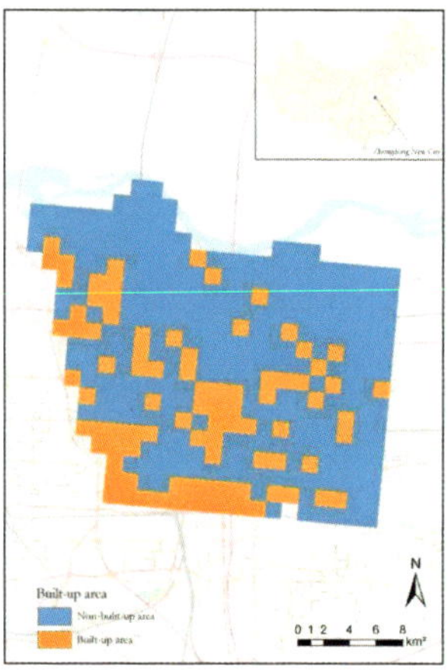

Built-up area

Non-built-up area

Built-up area

Figure 2.4 (a): Location of Zhengdong New City with nighttime light radiance

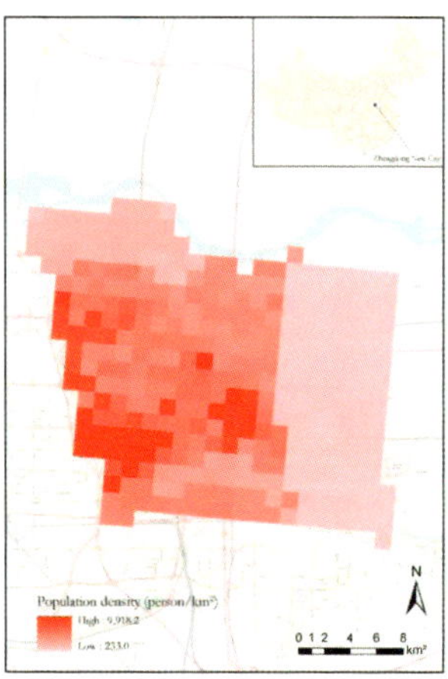

Population density (person/km²)

High: 9,918.2

Low: 233.0

Figure 2.4 (c): Location of Zhengdong New City with population density

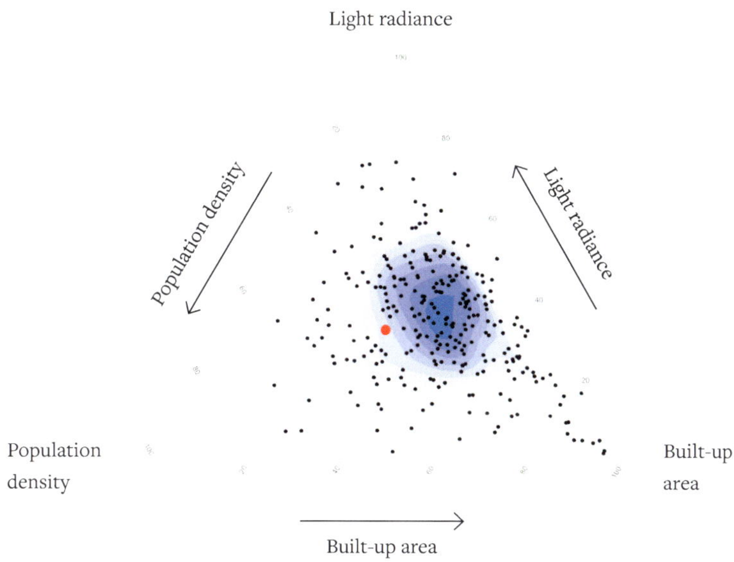

Figure 2.5: The distribution of new cities in a ternary contour
Notes: The central point is highlighted in red, representing the same degree of the relative percentages of these three components of urban vibrancy: built-up area, population density, and nighttime light radiance.

Relying on the ternary method, we further compare levels of urban vibrancy among new cities of different ages. We categorize these new city samples into three age groups: 0-5 years old, 5-10 years old, and more than 10 years old. We find that the older a new city is, the smaller the discrepancy is between its built-up area and the density of its human and economic activities. This justifies the proposition that city-making is a long-term game.

Why Are Some New Cities More Vibrant than Others?

According to the analysis above, there is a big variation in the vibrancy of new planned cities in China. Why are some new planned cities found to be more vibrant than others? This chapter responds to this question relying on two principal, theoretical economic theories relevant to urban vibrancy: location advantages and agglomeration economies. As mentioned above, we define urban vibrancy index as the distance between a point representing a city and the central point in the contour ternary.

Location Advantages

Urban economics argues that location is source of economic advantages such as high (or low) factor endowments of production and large (or small) accessibilities. Geographical location is one of the key decision-making determinants of firms and workers. In the literature, the advantages of location are found to account for a large portion of observed geographic concentration: such inherent geographic characteristics are measured as local agricultural productivity, access to natural resources, access to rivers or other transportation hubs (Bartik 1985; Carlton 1983; Ellison and Glaeser 1999). We thus propose that the level of vibrancy for a new city is highly positively related to its location.

For each new planned city, we consider three measures of location-related attractiveness for human and economic activities, including the new city's distance to the nearest airport, to the closest railway station, and to the city center. When the correlations between the urban vibrancy index and each one of these three measures of locational advantage are found to be positive for a given new city, then that new city with better access is said to be more vibrant.

The correlation between the urban vibrancy index and a single measure of location advantage is shown in Figure 2.6 (a), where the Euclidean distance (in absolute value) between the location of new planned city and the central point in the ternary contour is plotted against the distance to the nearest airport throughout all new city samples. The figure shows that a new planned city with better access to the airport is more vibrant. Figure 2.6 (b) and (c) illustrate similar patterns when we plot cross-city correlation between the index of urban vibrancy and two measures of location advantage, namely the distance to the closest railway station and to the city center. These findings support the explanation that a new planned city with more locational advantages is more favored by human and economic activities.

Forces of Agglomeration Economies

The agglomeration economies theory posits that workers and firms are likely to locate themselves in urban places that are dense, vibrant, and have mixed uses, in order to exploit agglomeration economies. The benefits of clustering different types of human and economic activities arise from knowledge spillovers, labor-market pooling, or the advantages of proximity of both suppliers and demanders in any economy with costly trade. There are two categories of agglomeration economies in the literature. One is localization economies created by co-locating firms within the same industry. The other is urbanization economies created by co-locating firms from different industries within the same city. Extant empirical studies provide evidence that urbanization economies are conducive to urban employment growth, especially in high-tech sectors (Combes 2000; Glaeser et al. 1992; V. Henderson,

Kuncoro, and Turner 1995; J. V. Henderson, Storeygard, and Weil 2012).

Based on agglomeration economies theory, we tested for the role of diversification in increasing urban vibrancy across new planned cities by plotting diversification, measured using the Herfindahl–Hirschman Index (*HHI*),[6] against urban vibrancy. The positive correlation is illustrated in Figure 2.6 (d), suggesting that a more diversified new city based on types of business scopes tends to attract more human and economic activities. Urban growth literature highlighting the importance of urbanization economies supports this finding.

Stages of Development

Theoretical models of satellite subcenter formation shed light on the role that the commuting costs play in altering the choices of firms and residents. Firms and residents have great incentives to locate outside of the CBD as large urban populations lead to high commuting cost. In line with these theoretical thoughts, when commuting costs for additional population or firms exceed the benefits, we may see the local demand for a new planned city outside the traditional core district. On the other hand, the long-term trends in urbanization suggest that urban areas are growing alongside the formation of new cities. The continuing flow of migrants into urban areas trigger a rise in land prices and motivate more developers to build urban projects, thereby increasing supply as newly added population and firms opt into new planned cities. We argue that a new planned city's urban vibrancy relates to the stages of development of the urban area where it is located. We define the stages of development as two dimensions leading to the formation of a new city: the core area's population density and its urbanization rate. We posit that a new city will be more vibrant if it is located in an urban area with both greater local population density and urbanization rate.

In the context of China, the growth of urban populations in cities is significantly limited by the household registration (*hukou*) system. This policy has been used to control rural-to-urban migration since the 1950s. One of the consequences of this system is the emergence of a huge number of under-urbanized cities in China (Au and Henderson 2006). Despite recent intensive efforts to relax controls over rural migration into the cities, urbanization rates for many Chinese cities are still lower

---

6. We measure a new city's (district's) diversification using the Herfindahl–Hirschman Index (HHI) as follows: $HHI_i=s_{ij}^2$ where s_{ij} is the share in city i of activity (business scope claimed by registered firms) j in local total number of activities. An increase in HHI reflects a lesser extent of diversification in a new city (district). We count the number of activities by taking advantage of business scope information from the registered companies dataset in China from 2009 to 2016. We summary the categories of activities extracting the key terms of business scope information and 30 types of activities are considered.

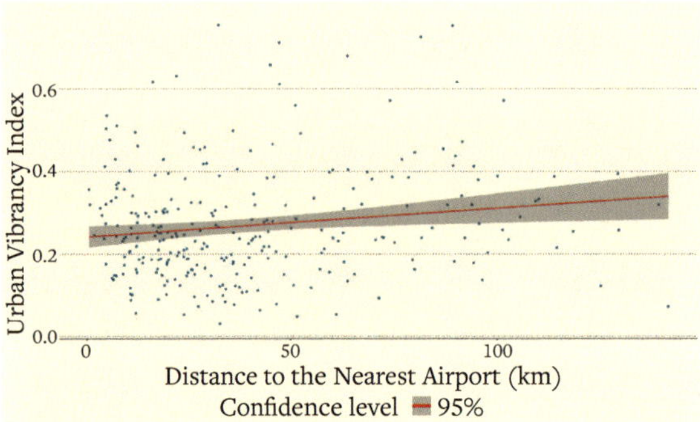

Figure 2.6 (a): Correlation between urban vibrancy and the distance to the airport

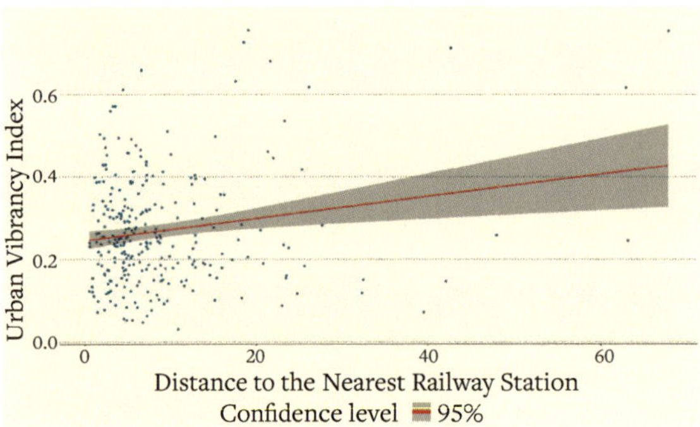

Figure 2.6 (b): Correlation between urban vibrancy and the distance to the closest railway station

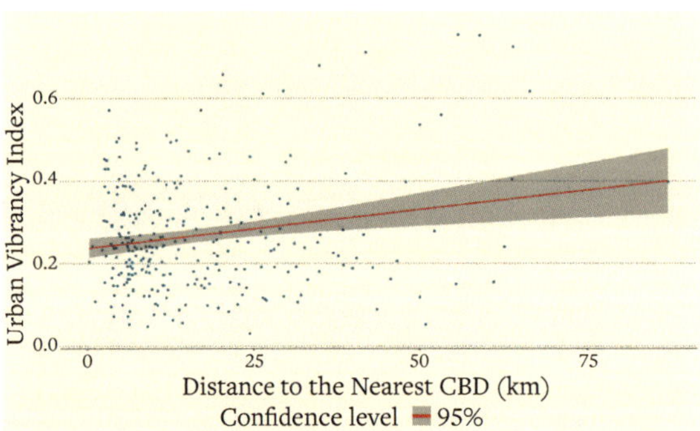

Figure 2.6 (c): Correlation between urban vibrancy and the distance to the CBD

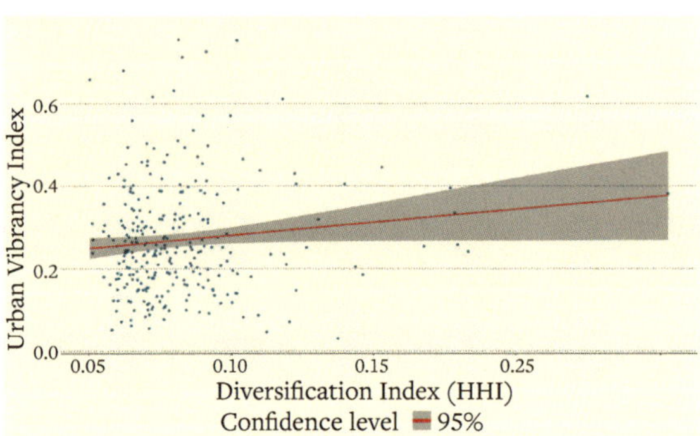

Figure 2.6 (d): Correlation between urban vibrancy and diversification

0.20

than analogous rates in other countries with similar productivity levels.

We highlight the role of stages of urban vibrancy development by illustrating a relationship: higher levels of urbanization, as measured as the percentage of the population living in urban areas, is positively associated with increasingly populated urban areas. Figure 2.7 plots the urbanized percentage for the host city where a new planned city was established against the population density at the core area of the host in the year where such new city was established. We illustrate such relationship using the first and fourth quartiles of new planned cities in terms of the magnitudes of urban vibrancy index. As illustrated in Figure 2.7, a large share of new planned cities with lower level of urban vibrancy lies below the regression trend line, suggesting that under-urbanization is perhaps due to *hukou* policy, which undermines the attractiveness of a new city as concerns human and economic activities. This pattern confirms the argument that a new planned city is likely to be more vibrant if it clusters varieties of economic activity and people as it grows in an urban area with high-density of population.

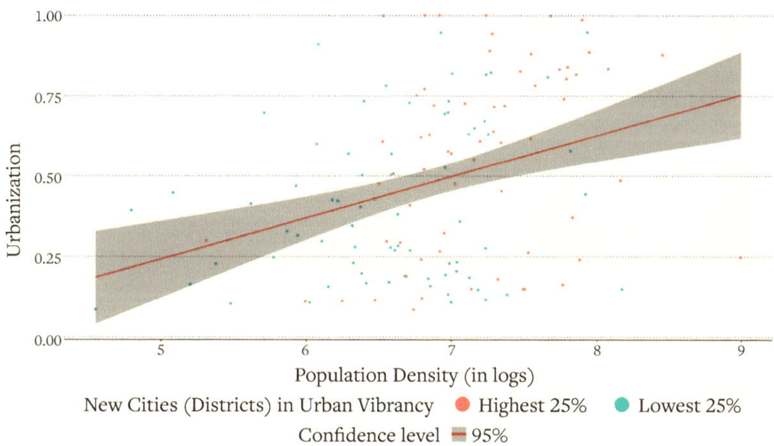

Figure 2.7: Urbanized percentage vs. Population density in the core area: The 25%highest and lowest vibrant new planned cities

Summary

The new planned city is one of the newest phenomena across Asian cities. It has accompanied the process of fast urbanization over the last decades especially in China. Using around 300 Chinese new planned cities since the early 1990s as our sample, we present the landscape of where these new planned cities are located. The data reveals that more than half of these new planned cities are located in coastal areas. Moreover, around one third of these new planned cities is found to be concentrated in metropolitan areas. We also identify the key industries, producer service, high-end manufacturing, and high-end service industries, located in these new planned cities by geocoding micro-level firms, supporting the argument that city mayors are attempting to make new economic space to accommodate urban based sectors as they are managing to upgrade the industrial structure.

We measure urban vibrancy across new planned cities using the method of ternary contour, in which the convergence of built-up area, population density, and the density of economic activity (indicated as light radiance) can be identified. Our analysis illustrates that some of the new planned cities in our sample are successfully attracting people and economic activities in their built-up areas, achieving a high level of urban vibrancy. On the other hand, the new planned cities with a low level of vibrancy are characterized by a high level of built-up area ratio, but a low level of population density or a low density of economic activity.

Using economic theories, we identify three factors that contribute to the increasing urban vibrancy of new planned cities: locational advantages with respect to external markets, forces of agglomeration economies generated from clustering diversified business activities, and stages of the development in the host areas. We find that human and economic activities favor being located in a new planned city that offers good access to transportation hubs (airports and railway) or closer to local central business district (CBD). Our analysis also presents evidence that a new planned city with a high level of diversification economies is made more vibrant by attracting high level of population and economic activities. In addition, we find that a new planned city is likely to be more vibrant thanks to a clustering of varieties of economic activity and people as it was built in a growing urban area with high density of population.

It is of great policy interest to predict the risks of younger new planned cities if they have similar attributes as those that have been established but are less vibrant. Local government officials were basically encouraged to increase GDP to comply with the national urbanization development by building new cities. But in many cases, firms and population were less likely to immediately flock to these new cities, generating empty cities that are home to more cranes than humans. To back such unprecedented proliferation of massive construction boom, local governments in China have racked up sizeable debt, generating great concerns among global investors and Chinese central government officials. Thus, failed new planned cities deserve more attention.

References

Au, Chun-Chung, and J. Vernon Henderson. 2006. "Are Chinese Cities Too Small?" *The Review of Economic Studies* 73 (3): 549–576.

Bartik, Timothy J. 1985. "Business Location Decisions in the United States: Estimates of the Effects of Unionization, Taxes, and Other Characteristics of States." *Journal of Business & Economic Statistics* 3 (1): 14–22.

Carlton, Dennis W. 1983. "The Location and Employment Choices of New Firms: An Econometric Model with Discrete and Continuous Endogenous Variables." *The Review of Economics and Statistics*, 440–449.

Chi, Guanghua, Yu Liu, Zhengwei Wu, and Haishan Wu. 2015. "Ghost Cities Analysis Based on Positioning Data in China." *ArXiv Preprint ArXiv:1510.08505*.

Combes, Pierre-Philippe. 2000. "Economic Structure and Local Growth: France, 1984–1993." *Journal of Urban Economics* 47 (3): 329–355.

Coulibaly, Souleymane, Uwe Klaus Deichmann, Maria Emilia Freire, Indermit S. Gill, Chorching Goh, Andreas Dietrich Kopp, Somik V. Lall, et al. 2008. "World Development Report 2009 : Reshaping Economic Geography." 43738. The World Bank. http://documents.worldbank.org/curated/en/730971468139804495/World-development-report-2009-reshaping-economic-geography.

Ellison, Glenn, and Edward L. Glaeser. 1999. "The Geographic Concentration of Industry: Does Natural Advantage Explain Agglomeration?" *American Economic Review* 89 (2): 311–316.

Glaeser, Edward L., Hedi D. Kallal, Jose A. Scheinkman, and Andrei Shleifer. 1992. "Growth in Cities." *Journal of Political Economy* 100 (6): 1126–1152.

Henderson, J. Vernon, Adam Storeygard, and David N. Weil. 2012. "Measuring Economic Growth from Outer Space." *American Economic Review* 102 (2): 994–1028.

Henderson, Vernon, Ari Kuncoro, and M. Turner. 1995. "Industrial Development in Cities. " *Journal of Political Economy* 103(5): 1067-1090.

Lai, Karen. 2012. "From 'Paris of the East'to 'New York of Asia'? The (Re) Development of Shanghai as a Financial Centre." In *New Economic Spaces in Asian Cities*, 168–183. Routledge.

Lowe, Matt. 2014. "Night Lights and ArcGis: A Brief Guide." *Avaliable Online: http:// economics. mit. edu/files/8945 (Accessed on 22 August 2014).*

OECD. 2015. *OECD Urban Policy Reviews: China 2015*. https://www.oecd-ilibrary.org/content/publication/9789264230040-en.

Shepard, Wade. 2015. *Ghost Cities of China: The Story of Cities without People in the World's Most Populated Country*. Zed Books Ltd.

Zhang, Qiming, Ying Zeng, Jinsong Deng, Ke Wang, Ruowei Jiang, and Ziran Ye. 2017. "'Ghost Cities' Identification Using Multi-Source Remote Sensing Datasets: A Case Study in Yangtze River Delta." *Applied Geography* 80:112-121.

Chapter 3.

Industrial Parks as a Major Type of New Cities in China: Measuring Production and Consumption Agglomeration Economies[1]

Siqi Zheng, Weizeng Sun, Jianfeng Wu, Matthew Kahn

Introduction

Over the last twenty years, place-based industrial policies have been a crucial component of the development strategy pursued by the Chinese government. China's local officials have allocated millions of acres of land and made huge capital investments to create new, "planned" cities. One of the major types of new cities is the type that grows out of industrial parks, which were initially planned to attract foreign direct investment (FDI) and create a local growth engine. As of 2006 there were 1,568 national-level and provincial-level industrial parks in more than 270 Chinese cities, covering 9,949 square kilometers in total. Although these parks only occupy about 0.1% of China's total land area, they contribute to about 10% of China's GDP and one-third of its FDI. Several studies have explored China's industrial parks and their positive impacts on local economies using a macro approach (Alder, Shao, and Zilibotti 2016; Schminke and Van Biesebroeck 2013; Wang 2013).

The spatial agglomeration literature has emphasized that such spillovers including input sharing, labor pooling, and knowledge spillovers, are often highly localized (Rosenthal and Strange 2003; 2004). It suggests that the spillovers of China's new industrial parks are likely to be localized within a city. In light of this, we will test for the effects of new parks on local production activity and on consumer behavior in a close proximity to the new parks. These new parks tend to be built at the edge of metropolitan areas, with low land rent, as well as tax, financial, and economic preferential policies to recruit highly productive firms. Physical proximity of firms wanting to co-agglomerate facilitates local, economic growth by stimulating trade thanks to lower transportation costs and easier learning and social interaction (Combes, Duranton, and Gobillon 2011). Moreover, these new industrial parks stimulate economic growth by solving a land assembly problem and a cross-firm coordination problem; they allow firms to come together in clusters in a timely fashion in the context of China. These benefits are more difficult to reap in developed-world cities that feature pre-existing durable structures and thousands of firms that do not fully consider the agglomeration's externalities when making their individual location choice. Successful industrial parks will attract skilled workers seek in a short commute to work. This creates an incentive for developers and retail businesses to open up quality housing and shopping close to the new parks. That's where a new edge city emerges.

This chapter builds on recent work that has documented the heterogeneous effects of place-based policies (Faggio, Silva, and Strange 2017). Several studies have examined the role of place-based policies on US local and regional growth, and their general

---

1. A longer version of this study, with complete models and empirical results, was published earlier (Zheng et al. 2017). We obtained the permission from the journal to re-use the paper here.

conclusion is that those place-based policies do not lead to net growth (Kline and Moretti 2014; Neumark and Kolko 2010; Rossi-Hansberg, Sarte, and Owens III 2010). As we report below, we find that 70% of the new industrial parks built during 1998-2007 in the eight major Chinese cities generate positive total factor productivity (TFP) spillovers in their vicinity, while 30% of those parks turn out to have negative or insignificant TFP spillovers.

This chapter uses detailed within-city, geocoded, micro data to study the consequences of Chinese local governments' recent investments in industrial parks. We document both the agglomeration benefits within a park's geographic area and those spillover effects beyond its boundaries. To empirically test for the extent of the localized agglomeration spillovers, we merge several geocoded data sets in eight Chinese major cities. These cities are home to 110 state- and provincial-level industrial parks. We test whether the creation of industrial parks is associated with production and consumption agglomerations based on key outcome indicators including: TFP for incumbent firms, local job and wage growth, new housing construction, home prices, and retail opportunities. This approach allows us to study the economic incidence of this public policy and builds on US work such as Busso, Gregory, and Kline (2013). These outcomes directly benefit local government officials because their fiscal revenue is tied to the commercial and residential land sales as well as to the tax collected from productive firms.

Our study builds on the research estimating localized productivity spillover effects. Previous studies on agglomeration more focus on the United States (Arzaghi and Henderson 2008; Greenstone, Hornbeck, and Moretti 2010; Rosenthal and Strange 2004). Our new estimates of the co-agglomeration effects build on the estimates from developed cities generated by Ellison, Glaeser and Kerr (2010). If place-based policies, such as industrial parks, help to reallocate labor and capital to their highest and best use, a local economic boom is likely to emerge.

Our work builds on the consumer city literature, which used data from the United States to highlight the emergent consumption opportunities available in cities (Diamond 2016; Glaeser, Kolko, and Saiz 2001; Handbury and Weinstein 2015). A new large industrial park creates a spatially concentrated center of employment and purchasing power away from the city center. Many of the workers in the park and at the expanding firms located close to the park will seek housing and shopping opportunities nearby. This creates a profit motive for retailers and housing developers to co-locate to supply such goods (Waldfogel 2008). We demonstrate that such positive, accumulative forces appear in the suburbs of China's major cities where new parks are created.

Industrial parks are not assigned to geographic locations at random: a mayor, for example, chooses whether and where to build an industrial park and then recruits firms to the park. To mitigate concerns of bias arising from park site selection, our study creates a control group of firms by identifying geographic site candidates for industrial parks based on urban planning documents from the 1950s to the early 1980s. The candidate areas that were not selected to become industrial parks form our control group. The research provides evidence of both production and consumption spillover effects of industrial parks: the clustering of private firms fosters higher levels of overall productivity, raising jobs and wages in the parks and nearby. Increased market potential, triggered by total income and employment growth in the vicinity of economic zones, creates incentives to build up new residential properties and other consumption amenities including retail shops and restaurants.

Using a micro databased approach, we further test for a rich set of such heterogeneous effects of industrial parks on local economic growth, and study the key mechanisms generating production and consumption spillovers. We find evidence of heterogeneous spillover effects such that older parks, state-level parks, parks have larger spillover effects. The parks featuring a higher human capital level, a larger share of FDI firms, a smaller share of State Owned Enterprises (SOEs), and a higher co-agglomeration level of industrial composition, are found to generate larger agglomeration effects. Moreover, parks with a better "fit" in the local incumbent industries (in terms of stronger input-output linkages, labor market pooling, and knowledge spillover) have generated more benefits on firms nearby.

This chapter is organized as follows: Sections 2 introduces the institutional background and the conceptual framework of our study. Section 3 presents the data and main results. We conclude in Section 4.

Institutional Background

This study focuses on industrial parks that the state or the provincial government in China authorized.[2] Being a host city of such parks has become a favorite strategy of city mayors to compete for FDI and foster local economic growth (Wu et al. 2013; Zheng et al. 2014). State and provincial governments approve plans for these parks, but most of them are implemented at the city level.

---

2. Industrial parks are authorized by different level governments: state, provincial, or prefecture (or lower) government. Those parks authorized by the state and provincial governments enjoy more favorable policies, such as lower interest rate loans, larger tax, land price, and utility price discounts. We focus only on those parks because many of the lower-level industrial parks did not obtain formal approval from the central and provincial governments and violated the relevant laws and regulations. In 2003 the central government investigated industrial parks regarding their potential violation of land use regulations, and this resulted in a large number of those lower-level industrial parks being abolished (see Cartier (2001) and Adler (2013)).

A two-step process opens China's industrial parks. Initially, a city government initiates an industrial park program accompanied by two general packages of policies. The first package amounts to the city government's large, capital investments to improve its transport infrastructure, utilities, storage, and other service facilities. Secondly, a separate bundle of preferential policies accompanies such city government development programs that includes: (1) tax deductions: corporate income tax rates of 15%-24% as opposed to the 33% firms normally pay in China are available to foreign enterprises, technologically-advanced enterprises, and export-oriented enterprises; (2) discounted land-use fees and utility prices: to attract productive firms, industrial parks set low, land-transfer fees and utility costs (electricity, water, etc.) as well as favorable payment methods; (3) special treatment in securing bank loans: state-owned banks prioritize and offer favorable interest rate for loan applications from the firms in industrial parks; and (4) faster and easier administrative approval registering firms engaged in exporting and importing.[3]

In the second step city mayors are likely to use a "managed hand" to promote its industrial park's policies. China's unique political system grants city mayors powers that far exceed their Western counterparts. On one hand, city governments representing the state own urban land. They can easily convert agricultural land at the edge of their cities into urban use. In addition, they have the power to allocate a large parcel of land to build an industrial park and engage in land assembly in ways that are impossible in the United States. Given that Chinese mayors improve their chances of promotion by increasing local economic growth, they have strong incentives to pursue pro-growth strategies. This, however, may also introduce the risk that some city mayors are not smart enough or too aggressive, for example, and end up making wrong decisions or over-investing in parks.

The recruitment process in industrial parks always operates at the lower, administrative committee (AC) level on behalf of the city government. The AC of an industrial park is responsible for directing and to administering the park— project approval, local taxation, land management, finance, personnel, and public service provision. Private negotiations take place between the AC staff members and the potential entrants regarding the exact bundle of subsidies each firm is to receive if it agrees to enter the park. These negotiations lead to a set of firms choosing to enter the park, at which point we observe the resulting outcomes both within and spilling over outside of the park. This recruitment process bears a close resemblance to the anchor-tenant recruitment challenge of creating a successful shopping mall (Pashigian and Gould 1998; Gould, Pashigian, and Prendergast 2005) and the

---

3. Incumbent firms within the park's boundary (established before the park was introduced), are generally unable to enjoy the favorable policies unless the park's administrative committee (AC) re-signs an agreement with them to change their registration status. Our interviews with some AC officials show that the latter case seldom happened.

development of suburban planned towns in the US (Henderson and Mitra 1996). The mall owners reap profit from activities within their mall but not from positive spillover effects into the local community. In contrast, in China city mayors are in charge of the entire jurisdiction (both the center city and the new city around the park) and thus internalizes all of the spillover effects generated by an industrial park. Although Chinese mayors seek to engage in pro-growth strategies, industrial parks are risky and costly. We will now turn to documenting how China's mayors go about navigating their risks.

China's mayors face capital constraints. Deciding whether and then where to invest in an industrial park, city mayors face a trade-off between the stream of benefits an industrial park promises and the upfront and opportunity costs of establishing the park on a large plot of land.[4] City mayors tend to raise funds through various channels including debt financing.[5] In 2011 the total fixed asset investment in 131 state-level industrial parks was RMB 2092 billion (USD $332), which was about 35% of the total fixed asset investment in the whole nation (*Zhong Guo Kai Fa Qu Nian Jian 2012* [*Yearbook of China Development Zone 2012*)] 2013). According to IMF estimates, local government debt reached 36% of GDP in 2013, a doubling since 2008, and will increase to 52% of GDP in 2019. Global investors have worried that such rising debt combined with a slowdown of the Chinese economy could create a future debt crisis ("Debt That Once Boosted Its Cities Now Burdens China" 2015). Such local debt crises are less likely to take place if past investments yield a significant flow of medium-term agglomeration benefits.

Data and Empirical Results

Our study focuses on eight major cities in China: Beijing, Shanghai, Shenzhen, Tianjin, Dalian, Wuhan, Xi'an, and Chengdu. We have the micro data sets of manufacturing firms, real estate transactions, and retail shops in those eight cities. These cities include all three first-tier cities in China (Beijing, Shanghai, Shenzhen) and several top-tier and second-tier cities. We construct four key geocoded data sets for these eight cities.

---

4. Such farmland is owned by rural villages. If the city government (the upper-level government of those rural villages) wants to build a new industrial park on farmland, it needs to convert the use-type of that land parcel from agricultural use to industrial use, and compensate the rural villages who own the land. In most cases the range of compensation for farmers for land taken is quite low because it is often based on income generated in agriculture use instead of being tied to its opportunity cost (the value of the land if allocated to urban use).

5. On average, bank loans, land sale revenue and on-budget fiscal revenue account for 28%, 25%, and 33% of the sources of municipal infrastructure investment in China in 2010, respectively, and the rest of the money comes from other non-bank, financial channels (Rutkowski 2013).

Three Geocoded Data Sets

- **The Industrial Parks Data Set**

According to the 2006 "Bulletin List for the Official Boundaries of Chinese Industrial Parks,"[6] there are 110 state- and provincial-level industrial parks in these eight cities (43 are state-level, and 67 are provincial-level), accounting for 8.6% of all such parks in China. From this list we know each park's name, location, and the year each was established. From the websites of industrial parks' ACs we obtain the exact geographic boundary of each park.[7] We then geocode the exact boundaries for the 110 parks in the eight cities (Figure 3.1). Each city has several industrial parks—Beijing has 21 parks, and Dalian has 8 parks. The average park's size is 11.88 square kilometers.[8]

- **The Manufacturing Plants Data Set** (ASIFs)

We obtain plant-level data from the Annual Survey of Industrial Firms (ASIFs) dataset of of the National Bureau of Statistics of China (NBSC) from 1998 to 2007. We link manufacturing plants over time using its information regarding ID numbers, names, industry codes, addresses (small zone/zone identifier), etc., and construct an unbalanced panel of 64,759 plants in this ten-year period for these eight cities. An advantage of this ASIFs data set is that it enables us to estimate total factor productivity (TFP) at the plant level. The second key variable is the wage measure at the plant level. The third variable is the park-specific, co-agglomeration index, which measures the extent to which two industries tend to co-locate. Higher co-agglomeration index means that the industries in the park enjoy a higher synergy.

- **The Housing and Consumption Retail Data Sets**

We obtain the price and quantity data for all newly-built residential complexes developed by real estate developers from 2006 to 2013 from the eight cities' local housing authorities. Across the eight cities, the number of observations varies from 8,000 to 40,000 complex-months.

We construct a dataset for local, private consumption goods based on dianping.com, *the Chinese analog of* yelp.com in the US. Dianping.com covers information on twelve general categories of urban consumption services, of which the three biggest

---

6. This information is provided by the Ministry of Land and Resources of China (MLRC).
7. For those parks that do not have websites or public released information, we contacted the local officials to obtain the boundary information.
8. The largest park is 64 square kilometers and the smallest one 0.2 square kilometers. If we measure the distance from the centroid of a park to the corresponding city's Central Business District, the average park is located 24.9 kilometers away. The farthest park is 95.1 kilometers from the city center.

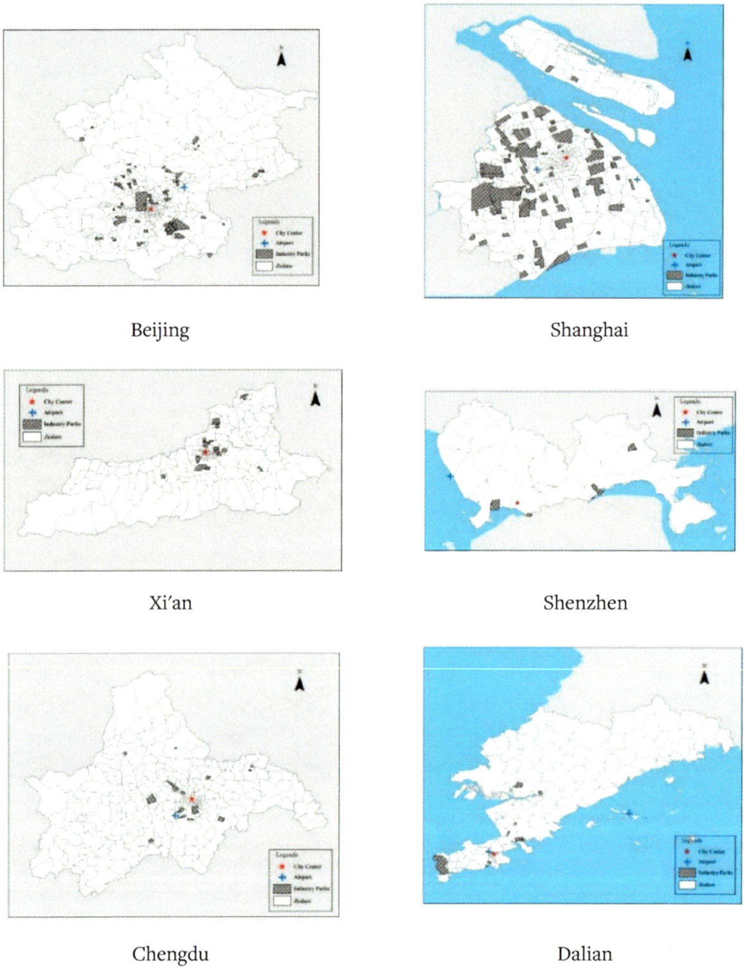

Figure 3.1: Within-city Locations and Geographic Boundaries of Industry Parks

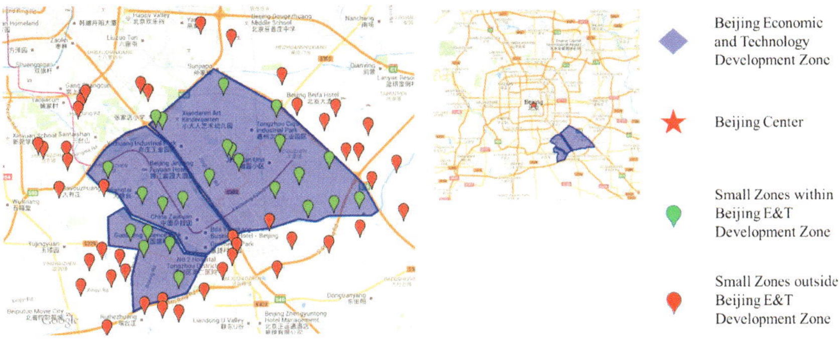

Figure 3.2: Geographic Unit of Analysis

are restaurants, entertainment facilities, and retail shops. For these three major categories, there were more than 874,000 retail establishments in these eight cities as of 2013. We know the establishment date for each shop.

Using a major industrial park in Beijing, the "Beijing Economic and Technological Development Zone," as an example, Figure 3.2 shows the above geographic units of analysis we use when doing the geocoding work. It presents the variable definitions and summary statistics. It also provides information concerning our various geographic levels of aggregation.

Main Results

- **Productivity Gain and Spillovers**

Using our econometric modeling approach, we observe a roughly 20% productivity premium on plant TFP thanks to being in a new park. We also find that plants located in the "impact area" of new parks—within 2 km of the park's boundary—experience a 10% increase in TFP. This is evidence of the positive spatial spillover effect, whose size is about half of the park's own TFP premium. We find similar, positive effects for wage gains at 7% for new park plants and at 4.4% for impact area plants.

- **Consumption Spillovers**

On average the spatial boundary of the impact area is 8 km from the park's boundary for new home sales, and 5 km from the park's boundary for openings of new restaurants, entertainment facilities, and retail shops. All else being equal, home prices are roughly 12% higher in the vicinity of an industrial park. The counts of new home sales, new restaurants, entertainment facilities, and retail shops also rise sharply in the vicinity of the park—43%, 51%, 39%, and 50% more than in a comparable place.

Based on the results reported above, we calculate the rough benefits the local government could gain by building an industrial park. The land value premium in this average park's impact area is about RMB 23 billion. Given Chinese land market rules, this is a onetime payment, but it is quite large as that amount equals 33% of the average city's annual fiscal revenue flow in the year 2007. The land where the park is placed could have been auctioned off as residential and commercial real estate. Using standard, hedonic pricing methods, we estimate the opportunity cost of the average park's land to be RMB 4.1 billion.[9] This opportunity cost underestimates the total cost of the park because there are other, often hidden costs. It is difficult to obtain the cost parameters of infrastructure investment and tax, and utility subsidies for building an industrial park because such cost information hidden by local governments. Our interview with an officer at National Development and Reform Commission of China (NDRC) gives us a rough estimate of 2.5 billion RMB of such costs for an average park in those cities. Combining the above costs, such costs only account for 28.7% of the land value premium in the park's impact area. Therefore, even without counting the long-term annual flows of tax revenue from firms, the huge net benefit from land sales (land value premium in the impact area minus the opportunity land cost within the park) already creates incentives for mayors to build industrial parks. But, of course, such huge land sale revenue depends on the park's success generating productivity gains. Since China's mayors face term limits with an average term-length running to around four years, the up-front land revenue incentives may even be stronger than collecting an annual, long-term flow of tax revenue from manufacturing firms.

- **Heterogeneity Effect**

In Figure 3.3 we graph the treatment effects for 40 parks sorted from lowest to highest effects, and we observe their productivity before and after the park was built based on our econometric model.

Figure 3.3 highlights the fact that some of the parks have a negative, but statistically insignificant, effect on plant productivity. If we count numbers, 75% of the new parks

---

9. The land sale revenue from residential and commercial land auctions in the park's vicinity is much larger. Here we estimate the residential land sale revenue to give an example. Our estimates show that the average industrial park increases home prices in its vicinity by 11.7%. We assume that land prices increase by the same rate. We obtain the land sale auction price data for the year 2007 and use the spatial gradient estimated from the housing price hedonic regression to predict the price of land across the city. We acknowledge that we do not take general equilibrium effect into account here, and we use post-improvement prices (after the public project investment) instead of pre-improvement prices when conducting the estimation. On the cost side, to attract productive firms, local governments always sell the industrial land within the park to them at very low, subsidized prices, and in some cases even at a price of zero. We estimate the opportunity cost of this favorable land subsidy by calculating the market value of the land within the park if it could have been developed into residential uses (assuming zero prices for industrial uses). This subsidy is valued at RMB 4.1 billion for the average park.

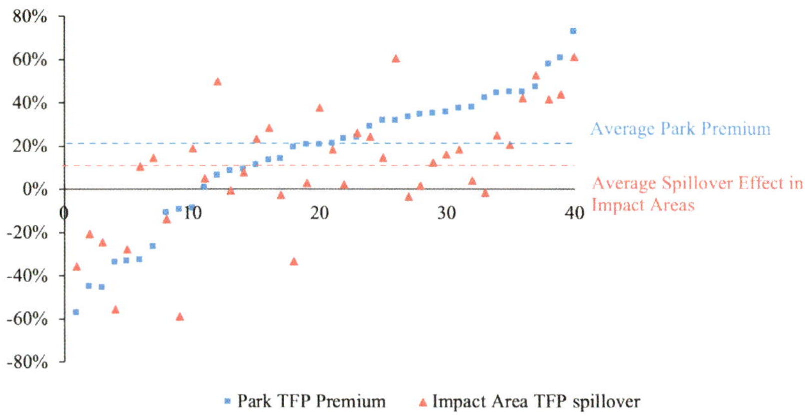

Figure 3.3: Estimating the TFP Premium for Each of the Forty New Parks

built during 1998-2007 in the eight cities generate positive TFP premiums within the park's boundary; whereas 25% of parks turns out to have negative TFP premiums. Regarding TFP spillovers to nearby incumbent firms, 70% of the parks have positive spillovers, and 30% have negative spillovers (most of the negative coefficients are insignificant).

We find that older parks do have larger productivity spillovers. As time passes, the spillovers for both old and new parks become larger. We interpret this as evidence of a multiplier effect. We also find that the state-level parks generate larger TFP spillovers than provincial-level parks, but wage spillovers in them is similar. We also observe that parks featuring a higher share of human capital, a higher foreign direct investment, and higher co-agglomeration effects within the park all have a higher spillover effects. A ten percentage point increase in the share of park workers who are college graduates is associated with a 26% increase in the TFP spillover in the impact area.

On the consumption side, all else being equal, for state-level parks and parks featuring more human capital, greater co-agglomeration, more FDI, and fewer SOEs, we find larger spillover impacts on nearby housing construction, home prices, and new retail openings. These results support our claim that parks have heterogeneous impacts and that the composition of these parks plays a key role. The finding that the co-agglomeration index has a positive spillover effect in both the TFP and the consumer city regressions supports the claim that this is new synergistic activity rather than simply a reshuffling of economic activity that would have taken place somewhere in the same city in the absence of the park's creation.

Conclusion

This chapter provides strong support for Marshallian theories of localized production and consumption agglomeration in a leading developing country. Using the opening of 110 industrial parks across eight major Chinese cities, we quantify the spillover effects on productivity, manufacturing employment, incumbent firm survival, real estate construction, real estate pricing, and retail store openings for economic activity close to these new suburban centers of productivity. Consistent with Marshall's core hypotheses, we find that proximity to the parks facilitates trade and growth because such co-agglomeration reduces the costs of moving goods, people, and ideas.

We have also documented that the parks differ with respect to their productive spillover effects. A recent article in macroeconomics measures the productivity wedges across Chinese firms (see Hsieh and Klenow (2009)). This research argues that government-induced distortions act like a subsidy for unproductive firms. For example, state-owned enterprises receive special treatment, receiving cheaper land and capital access. Our results indicate that government policies that encourage the creation of high human capital industrial parks are more likely to facilitate productivity growth.

Unlike previous evaluations of government subsidies for place-based programs, we have explicitly measured impacts for both the production and consumption sides of the economy. A new park creates a spatially concentrated increase in local market potential as well paid workers seek nearby housing and retail opportunities. Given that Chinese urbanites spend a great deal of time commuting to work, household quality of life improves with suburban employment options that enable much shorter commutes and allow them to shop and generally live more easily. Unlike in the classic monocentric Chinese city, this means that the new parks lead to sharp improvements in its workers' quality of life, and this ought to attract talented workers to seek these jobs (Duranton and Turner 2011; Monte, Redding, and Rossi-Hansberg 2018).

Our results also show that not all industrial parks are successful, even in our sample of 110 parks among the first-tier cities and relatively large cities.[10] The geographic spillover effect of parks is an increasing function of the park's overall human capital level, the FDI share, the SOE share, and its synergy with nearby incumbent firms.

---

10. If data permits, this study should be expanded to less developed cities to see if industry parks' positive impacts diminish when this policy extends down the hierarchy of cities. We tried our best but still cannot obtain this micro-level firm data beyond these eight cities. Therefore, we view this to be a valuable future research topic. In the conclusion, we mention the possibility that if we look at relatively small cities and those cities in China's middle and western regions, it is possible that the probability of less successful or unsuccessful parks would emerge.

Nevertheless, on average, we do find positive production and consumption spillovers. Other studies on China's industrial parks also confirm such positive impacts on local economic growth. It is interesting, therefore, to understand why this place-based policy did not work well in many developed countries (Busso, Gregory, and Kline 2013; Glaeser and Gottlieb 2008; Papke 1994), but has an optimistic outcome in China. We propose two possible (and speculative) explanations: First, in developed countries, place-based policies often target regions that lag behind others. China's industrial park policy incorporates motivations of efficiency and equity with the additional goal of experimenting with market reforms. On the efficiency side, industrial parks pursue a reduction of preexisting distortions in the old, central planning regime and the exploitation of agglomeration effects (Alder, Shao, and Zilibotti 2016). Second, the active role of the government has been crucial for China's development because it supported a fast move towards more modern and productive sectors that they believe would have positive externalities on the whole economy (Rodrik 2006). In our case, the "managed hand" of Chinese city governments solves a land assembly problem and a cross-firm coordination problem, allowing firms to cluster in a timely fashion, which is unimaginable in cities featuring preexisting, durable structures. It may also not be possible in a US city where such projects would face more "Not In My Back Yard" (NIMBY) opposition.

References

Adler, Solomon. 2013. *The Chinese Economy*. Routledge.

Alder, Simon, Lin Shao, and Fabrizio Zilibotti. 2016. "Economic Reforms and Industrial Policy in a Panel of Chinese Cities." *Journal of Economic Growth* 21 (4): 305–349.

Arzaghi, Mohammad, and J. Vernon Henderson. 2008. "Networking off Madison Avenue." *The Review of Economic Studies* 75 (4): 1011–1038.

Busso, Matias, Jesse Gregory, and Patrick Kline. 2013. "Assessing the Incidence and Efficiency of a Prominent Place Based Policy." *American Economic Review* 103 (2): 897–947.

Cartier, Carolyn. 2001. "'Zone Fever', the Arable Land Debate, and Real Estate Speculation: China's Evolving Land Use Regime and Its Geographical Contradictions." *Journal of Contemporary China* 10 (28): 445–469.

Combes, Pierre-Philippe, Gilles Duranton, and Laurent Gobillon. 2011. "The Identification of Agglomeration Economies." *Journal of Economic Geography* 11 (2): 253–266.

"Debt That Once Boosted Its Cities Now Burdens China." 2015. WSJ. January 28, 2015. https://www.wsj.com/articles/debt-that-once-boosted-its-cities-now-burdens-china-1422415981.

Diamond, Rebecca. 2016. "The Determinants and Welfare Implications of US Workers' Diverging Location Choices by Skill: 1980-2000." *American Economic Review* 106 (3): 479–524.

Duranton, Gilles, and Matthew A. Turner. 2011. "The Fundamental Law of Road Congestion: Evidence from US Cities." *American Economic Review* 101 (6): 2616–52.

Ellison, Glenn, Edward L. Glaeser, and William R. Kerr. 2010. "What Causes Industry Agglomeration? Evidence from Coagglomeration Patterns." *American Economic Review* 100 (3): 1195–1213.

Faggio, Giulia, Olmo Silva, and William C. Strange. 2017. "Heterogeneous Agglomeration." *Review of Economics and Statistics* 99 (1): 80–94.

Glaeser, Edward L., and Joshua D. Gottlieb. 2008. "The Economics of Place-Making Policies." *Brookings Papers on Economic Activity*, 155–239.

Glaeser, Edward L., Jed Kolko, and Albert Saiz. 2001. "Consumer City." *Journal of Economic Geography* 1 (1): 27–50.

Gould, Eric D., B. Peter Pashigian, and Canice J. Prendergast. 2005. "Contracts, Externalities, and Incentives in Shopping Malls." *Review of Economics and Statistics* 87 (3): 411–422.

Greenstone, Michael, Richard Hornbeck, and Enrico Moretti. 2010. "Identifying Agglomeration Spillovers: Evidence from Winners and Losers of Large Plant Openings." *Journal of Political Economy* 118 (3): 536–598.

Handbury, Jessie, and David E. Weinstein. 2015. "Goods Prices and Availability in Cities." *The Review of Economic Studies* 82 (1): 258–296.

Henderson, Vernon, and Arindam Mitra. 1996. "The New Urban Landscape: Developers and Edge Cities." *Regional Science and Urban Economics* 26 (6): 613–643.

Hsieh, Chang-Tai, and Peter J. Klenow. 2009. "Misallocation and Manufacturing TFP in China and India." *The Quarterly Journal of Economics* 124 (4): 1403–1448.

Kline, Patrick, and Enrico Moretti. 2014. "Local Economic Development, Agglomeration Economies, and the Big Push: 100 Years of Evidence from the Tennessee Valley Authority." *The Quarterly Journal of Economics* 129 (1): 275–331.

Monte, Ferdinando, Stephen J. Redding, and Esteban Rossi-Hansberg. 2018. "Commuting, Migration, and Local Employment Elasticities." *American Economic Review* 108 (12): 3855–90.

Neumark, David, and Jed Kolko. 2010. "Do Enterprise Zones Create Jobs? Evidence from California's Enterprise Zone Program." *Journal of Urban Economics* 68 (1): 1–19.

Papke, Leslie E. 1994. "Tax Policy and Urban Development: Evidence from the Indiana Enterprise Zone Program." *Journal of Public Economics* 54 (1): 37–49.

Pashigian, B. Peter, and Eric D. Gould. 1998. "Internalizing Externalities: The Pricing of Space in Shopping Malls." *The Journal of Law and Economics* 41 (1): 115–142.

Rodrik, Dani. 2006. "What's so Special about China's Exports?" *China & World Economy* 14 (5): 1–19.

Rosenthal, Stuart S., and William C. Strange. 2003. “Geography, Industrial Organization, and Agglomeration.” *Review of Economics and Statistics* 85 (2): 377–393.

Rosenthal, Stuart S., and William C. Strange. 2004. “Evidence on the Nature and Sources of Agglomeration Economies.” In *Handbook of Regional and Urban Economics*, 4:2119–2171. Elsevier.

Rossi-Hansberg, Esteban, Pierre-Daniel Sarte, and Raymond Owens III. 2010. “Housing Externalities.” *Journal of Political Economy* 118 (3): 485–535.
Rutkowski, Ryan. 2013. “Four Myths about Local Infrastructure Investment in China.” PIIE. October 2, 2013. https://www.piie.com/blogs/china-economic-watch/four-myths-about-local-infrastructure-investment-china.

Schminke, Annette, and Johannes Van Biesebroeck. 2013. “Using Export Market Performance to Evaluate Regional Preferential Policies in China.” *Review of World Economics* 149 (2): 343–367.

Waldfogel, Joel. 2008. “The Median Voter and the Median Consumer: Local Private Goods and Population Composition.” *Journal of Urban Economics* 63 (2): 567–582.

Wang, Jin. 2013. “The Economic Impact of Special Economic Zones: Evidence from Chinese Municipalities.” *Journal of Development Economics* 101: 133–147.

Wu, Jing, Yongheng Deng, Jun Huang, Randall Morck, and Bernard Yeung. 2013. No. 18754 “Incentives and Outcomes: China’s Environmental Policy.” National Bureau of Economic Research. NBER Working Paper No. 18754

Zheng, Siqi, Matthew E. Kahn, Weizeng Sun, and Danglun Luo. 2014. “Incentives for China’s Urban Mayors to Mitigate Pollution Externalities: The Role of the Central Government and Public Environmentalism.” *Regional Science and Urban Economics* 47: 61–71.

Zheng, Siqi, Weizeng Sun, Jianfeng Wu, and Matthew E. Kahn. 2017. “The Birth of Edge Cities in China: Measuring the Effects of Industrial Parks Policy.” *Journal of Urban Economics* 100: 80–103.

Zhong Guo Kai Fa Qu Nian Jian 2012 [*Yearbook of China Development Zone 2012*)]. 2013. China Financial & Economic Publishing House.

Chapter 4.

Financing New Cities in China: Historical Evolution and Future Aspiration

Manish Srivastava, Wingshan Yip

Cross the river by stepping on one stone at a time.
Deng Xiao Ping

China's urbanization and the financing of its new cities is a story of resourcefulness and experimentation amalgamated with boundless ambition. Since the last quarter of the twentieth century, Asia has been at the forefront of rapid urbanization, and China has led the way. China's urban population has increased from 10% of the country's total population in the early 1950s to more than 50% by 2010, and it is estimated to be almost 59% in 2018,[1] with 700 million people now living in urban centers. Another 300 million people are expected to migrate from rural to urban centers in the next two decades. The working age population in China declined to 71.2% in 2018 after peaking at 73.8% in 2010. China's share of the population of people who are 65 years and older has risen rapidly from 5.7% in 1990 to 11.2% in 2018.[2]

Rural-urban migration and demographic shifts are contributing to a profound reorganization of Chinese society, as is evident from its emerging urban governance structures; the distribution of administrative decision-making at the central and local government[3] levels; emerging mechanisms to bridge the expanding fiscal gaps, especially at the local government levels; policy designs to address the growing economic inequality between the urban-migrants and residents who already have urban *Hukou*;[4] and the emerging consensus of pursuing inclusive and sustainable economic paradigms, with the objective of building a harmonious and creative society.

In the following discussion we highlight the evolution of the financial underpinnings of new city developments in China in its pursuit of rapid urbanization and explore the way forward.

---

1. *Source:* World Bank Data
2. *Source:* World Bank Data
3. According to the China Statistical Yearbook 2019, the whole country is divided into provinces, autonomous regions and municipalities directly under the Central Government. Provinces and autonomous regions are further divided into autonomous prefectures, counties, autonomous counties and cities. Autonomous prefectures are further divided into counties, autonomous counties and cities. Counties and autonomous counties are further divided into townships, ethnic townships and towns. Municipalities directly under the Central Government and large cities are divided into districts and counties. It is also mentioned that the State shall, when necessary, establish special administrative regions ("China Statistical Yearbook 2019" n.d.).
4. As defined in the "Notes" section of Urban China by Xuefei Ren, Hukou is the household registration system instituted in the 1950s that divides the national population of China into urban and rural sectors (Ren 2013).

The First Phase of Financing New Cities in China

An export-led, industrial strategy aimed at increasing GSDP[5] and GDP[6] growth rates and consequently alleviating poverty drove the first phase of China's urbanization. After Chairman Deng Xiao Ping's visit to the United States in 1978, China opened up to the world. Policymakers recognized China's inherent, comparative advantage arising from its access to abundant natural resources, access to large pools of labor, internationally competitive labor costs, its large population of potential consumers, and the capacity of the unitary state to facilitate assembling these factors of production to harness the economic benefits from large scale modernization[7] and industrialization.

China became open to foreign direct investment (FDI) in 1979.[8] Between 1979 and 2008, the cumulative FDI in China amounted to USD 0.9 trillion spread over 660,127 projects ("China Statistical Yearbook-2014" n.d.). During this period China's GDP grew from USD 178.3 billion to USD 4.6 trillion and to USD 13.6 trillion in 2018.[9] The trajectory of this GDP expansion implied an annual average growth rate of 11.8% between 1979 and 2018. The confluence of China's comparative advantages and its newfound access to international capital became the underlying narrative of its first phase of industrialization. China's new city developments have been the playground of its rapid industrialization strategy.

Land-use Revenue Monetization

In their pursuit of developing new cities, China's policymakers were able to tap into a unique feature of China's politico-economic system: the *State*[10] owns the land in urban areas, and rural collectives own the land in the rural areas. Private ownership of land is not permitted in China. In the Chinese socialist system, land is considered a common good, the benefits of which are meant to be collectively shared with all citizens (i.e. administered by the state as the representative of its entire citizenry) rather than with a few private owners.

In contrast, once land is released into private ownership in Western countries, it typically operates to serve private interests except for land acquired through eminent

---

5. Gross State Domestic Product
6. Gross Domestic Product
7. Modernization of industry, science & technology, agriculture, and national defense formed the core deliberations at the 3rd Plenary Session of the Central Committee of the CCP in 1979.
8. China opened up for foreign direct investment after the adoption of the Law of the People's Republic of China on Joint Ventures Using Chinese and Foreign Investment in 1979.
9. *Source:* World Bank Data
10. The term State here represents the politico-economic entity of which the governments (both Central and Local) represent the administrative component.

domain. The ownership of land can typically change hands freely. Consequently, the benefits of increases in land values mostly accrue to the private owners of land and only somewhat across time to the local governments in the form of higher property taxes. In China, since all urban land is exclusively owned by the State, there remains room in the future for market-based repricing (both price and terms) of those land-use rights as it comes due for renewal.

Without the ability to sell land outright, local governments in China monetized the ownership of land through the sale of land-use rights for industrial, commercial, and residential development activities,[11] as well as for infrastructure development projects. Land-use rights are sold in exchange for one-time, upfront cash payments. Until 2007 the payments thus received accrued to the local governments and were counted as *off budgetary* receipts, i.e. they are kept out of consideration in the regular budget. Since 2007, however, these receipts are included as part of the regular budget.

During the 1990s, as various provinces and their sub-provincial governments competed with one another to attract industrial activity and FDI to their respective areas, offering the use of land at prices that often were significantly below market value became a tactical tool and even the norm for local governments. Land-use rights within urban centers were typically sold for residential and commercial developments.

At the urban periphery, however, local governments acquired land from the rural collectives at low cost, converted it to industrial use, and then sold the rights to use the land to investors in industrial activity. Simultaneously, local governments encouraged labor from rural areas to migrate and reside nearer these new centers of industrial activity to generate an efficient and regular supply of low-cost labor. These advantages meant retaining and generating even more industrial activity, therefore resulting in a horizontal expansion of urban areas at the periphery of existing cities, igniting the development of many new cities, and resulting in turn in the *urban sprawl* we see in China today (Rithmire 2015).

The sale of land-use rights generates cash revenue that is mainly used for compensation for land acquisition and demolition, land development expenditure, agricultural expenditure, and urban construction expenditure ("Guo Wu Yuan Ban Gong Ting Guan Yu Gui Fan Guo You Tu Di Shi Yong Quan Chu Rang Shou Zhi Guan Li De Tong Zhi [Notice of the General Office of the State Council, PRC]" 2006). Local governments also use revenue from the sale of the land-use rights to provide

11. Land-use rights in China are typically sold for a period of thirty and forty years for industrial and commercial uses respectively, and for seventy years for residential use. Regulations pertaining to the duration of the land-use right are still emerging China, particularly for situations involving multiple or mixed-uses.

infrastructure for new cities and to maintain and operate any in-place infrastructure. From 2008 to 2013 the total land-leasing fee (rent) received by the government was around $2.2 trillion, while urban development expenditure accounted for 69.7% of the total non-cost[12] expenditure (Zheng, Shi, and Wu 2014).

China is unique in the way revenues and expenditures are aligned at the central and local government levels. Local governments in China receive 50% of the country's fiscal revenues and are responsible for 80% of the spending (Frey et al. 2014), leaving a large fiscal gap. Local governments are responsible for expenditures such as provision of maintenance of its area's infrastructure, pensions,[13] healthcare, etc. Revenue collections at the central level are allocated to provincial governments and through them to the local governments via a complex set of direct, indirect, and grant-based channels.

For local governments and their leaders, who are appointed by the Chinese Communist Party (CCP), typically for up to five years and whose career trajectory is measured according to their proven ability to deliver rapid GDP growth, the off-budget revenues that land-use monetization generates have been a valuable source of added fiscal flexibility. As a result, the sale of land-use rights became the predominant, financing instrument during the first phase of China's new city developments.

Land-use monetization, however, has its limitations, and these came to light as the global economy slowed in the aftermath of the 2008 global financial crisis. The first limitation is that sustained land-use monetization on the periphery of urban centers leads to sprawl and contributes to the need for even more investment in infrastructure to connect these new cities at the periphery to other parts of the existing urban core and to other new cities in the region. Secondly, revenues from land-use monetization can be volatile and can therefore leave unexpected deficits needed to service local government's fiscal needs. Thirdly, since the revenues generated from land-use monetization happen only once, even more land-use needs to be monetized just to maintain and operate the infrastructure provided to service the industrial, commercial, and residential activities already incurred with the previous sale of land-use rights. This in itself is fiscally unsustainable.
To maintain the momentum of economic growth in the aftermath of the global financial crisis of 2008, with the major markets for China's exports in deep slowdown, the central government injected a powerful fiscal stimulus package.

---

12. Cost expenditure includes the cost of land acquisition, demolition and land development. All other expenditures are considered non-cost expenditure.
13. According to the World Bank databank, life expectancy at birth in China in 1978 when reforms started was 66.4 years and by 2017 it increased to 76.4 years, an increase of 15.1%. This obviously increases the burden of pension payments for the local governments.

The Second Phase of Financing New Cities in China

The second phase of China's urbanization followed the contours of the shift of China's national development policy framework away from a predominantly export-led economic growth model towards one focused on expanding domestic consumption as the principal driver of future GDP growth. This reorientation of national policy put the spotlight on reaping the rich benefits that had accrued from the first phase of new city developments. China had substantially urbanized, and its urban consumers had amassed sizeable disposable incomes and savings.[14]

Even as the world's other large economies struggled to recover from the significant slowdown, China accelerated its new city development efforts by first consolidating and then also expanding options for their financing. Land-use monetization revenues, which had been off-budget, were now brought on-budget and consolidated into the local government's regular financing structures. The financing options were also expanded to include some combination of (i) indirect borrowing in the form of Local Government Financing Vehicles (LGFVs);[15] (ii) direct borrowings in the form of Local Government (Municipal) Bonds; and (iii) pooling capital and expertise through partnerships with private capital providers and developers and building Public-Private Partnerships (PPPs). These options and their implications are examined below.

Local Government Financing Vehicles (LGFVs)

Indirect land borrowing is considered to be the supplementary financing method for land leasing. Local governments borrow indirectly, through LGFVs, from bond markets or banks[16] and pledge the future revenues from selling land-use rights as collateral. LGFVs issue bonds known as LGFV Bonds or Chengtou Bonds. These bonds have been an important financial instrument in facilitating the creation of new cities in the second phase of China's urbanization. The issuance of these bonds has broadly mirrored the trajectory of planned area new cities in China.[17]

The market for these bonds grew dramatically after the Chinese government's fiscal stimulus of 2008 in response to the global financial crisis. As the pace of new city development gathered steam in China, the issuance of the LGFV Bonds accelerated

---

14. China's Gross Savings Rate as of December 2010 was at 51.5% and as of December 2018 was 45.7%. Gross Domestic Savings is calculated as Nominal GDP less Final Consumption Expenditure
Source: CEIC Data
15. LGFVs are also known as Urban Development Investment Corporations (or UDICs)
16. One major bank that lends out development bank loans to LGFVs is the China Development Bank.
17. Even after controlling a set of factors (including city density, productivity, etc.), the construction of a new city remains as a significant reason for the local government to issue LGFV bonds (Chang and Lu 2017).

in 2010. By 2012, however, because of the deteriorating credit quality of LGFV Bonds and concerns about the off-balance sheet treatment of LGFVs in general along with the implied lack of transparency and supervision (International Monetary Fund. Fiscal Affairs Dept. 2018), the central government was becoming increasingly concerned about the systemic risk these bonds posed for the Chinese economy.

One concern with LGFVs has been that the instrument uses revenue from future land-use right monetization as collateral. The reliance on future revenues to borrow now often creates cash flow (asset-liability) mismatches and, therefore, duration risk for local governments, impacting their ability to repay debt during times when they are most negatively affected. Indeed, the local governments' LGFV related liability exposure does not change even when housing prices and consequently land prices experience sudden drops, whether naturally or owing to policy changes adopted by the central government to manage national debt and/or to curtail housing price inflation.

The artificially inflated, short-term, municipal cash flows through increases in off-balance sheet indebtedness created fiscal hazards for local governments. Furthermore, since these instruments offer significantly higher yields (more than 10% in many cases) than ordinary bank deposits, they were highly attractive to retail investors who bought these instruments without fully understanding the substantial, underlying default risk. The size of LGFV Bonds grew to RMB 3.8 trillion by 2014. This was a 71% increase over 2013 and implied a twenty-fold increase relative to 2010. This rapid expansion of LGFV's, which remained off-budget, posed significant systemic risk.

The People's Bank of China (PBOC) responded to this growing exposure to LFGV risks by tactically replacing certain LGFV Bonds with bonds directly issued by the local governments in selected jurisdictions and by also inducing local governments to directly issue bonds backed by specific projects. When compared with the LGFV Bonds these replacement bonds better matched the duration of the cash in-flows from underlying projects with the cash out-flows of their respective borrowing instruments.

Local Government Bonds or Municipal Bonds

In 2015 the State Council of China first clarified that local governments be allowed to issue Local Government Bonds (LGBs). The LGBs were introduced in response to the risks of LGFV borrowings and generally as a more robust alternative to filling the fiscal gaps while remaining on local government balance sheets. A three-year, bond-swap program was also introduced by the central government to encourage local governments to replace the costly and short-term LGFV debts with the LGBs. Ever since the introduction of the bond-swap program, the LGFV Bond issuances have been moderate relative to the new LGB issuances.

According to China's 2018 Statistical Report, USD 1.8 trillion of LGBs were issued under the swap program to replace high-risk LGFV borrowings. Since 2015, the LGB issuances have exceeded LGFV Bond issuances[18] and have been instrumental in the development of new cities. Among the LGBs outstanding in 2018, 24% were associated with land borrowing, 17% with toll roads, 13% with transportation, and 7% with urban and rural infrastructure development ("Guang Fa Hong Guan: Shen Me Shi Zhuan Xiang Zhai? [GF Securities: What Is Special Purpose Fund?]" 2018). The maturity of LGBs can be as long as 20 years, whereas the average maturity of the outstanding LGBs is 4.5 years ("Chapter 5 Local Government Bonds" 2019).

Figure 4.1 shows that the LGBs have been increasingly accepted as an important financial instrument for financing new cities in China. The increasing acceptability of LGBs as a substitute for LGFV Bonds is reflected in the fact that between 2014 and 2018, the cost of financing for local governments has, on the average, dropped by 650 basis points. Since 2013, RMB 12.2 trillion of the debt has been replaced by LGBs ("2018 Nian Guo Min Jing Ji He She Hui Fa Zhan Tong Ji Gong Bao [2018 Statistical Communique On National Economic And Social Development]" 2019).

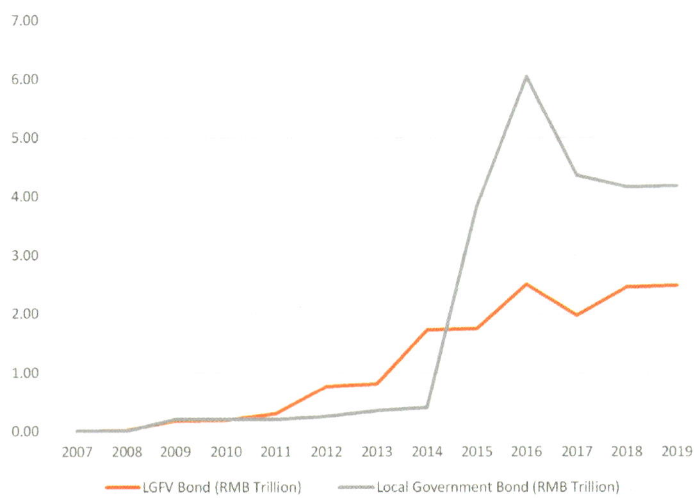

Figure 4.1: LGFV Bond vs LGB Issuances
Source: WIND Economic Database

18. However, the outstanding LGFV Bonds represent only a fraction of the overall LGFV's debt obligations, which also include bank loans and Build-Transfer financing.

Public Private Partnerships (PPPs)

PPPs are suitable when the existing fiscal revenues and the land-use rent earned by a local government are not adequate to fund new cities and large-scale urban developments. If a private-sector developer with sufficient funding capacity is interested in developing a large-scale urban project or a new city, it can partner with the local government. In this arrangement the government contributes land and the private developer funds the construction and the overall development. Equity ownership is shared between the parties to reflect their respective contributions. Future income and capital generated from the sale of assets is divided amongst the stakeholders, including the local government, in accordance with the terms of agreements.

For the local government, PPP is a financing method that raises capital from private companies based on the land values and future earnings from the new city developments. Besides financing, the private developer typically enhances the project's quality and chances of success through time-tested know-how, deployment of skilled teams supervised by experienced senior management, and insights into potential constraints and costless options based on their previous experience. Therefore, designing adequate and fair incentives for the various stakeholders with a focus on making the new city successful is a key imperative. A typical PPP contract can last twenty-five years or longer. PPP contracts have been used in large-scale, urban developments in new cities such as Suzhou Industrial Park and Gu'an New Industry City[19] as well as in existing urban centers such as Shanghai, Beijing, and Chongqing.

Since the financing sources for private developers are relatively limited and costly, developers are usually more willing to adopt new and creative financing solutions. For them, one traditional way is to borrow development loans from banks. The reputation of the developer and the new city determine the terms of the loan. Funds from trust companies are another major funding source for private developers because of their equity-like nature and comparatively easy accessibility; but trust products are often associated with higher financing costs and interest rates.

Apart from bank loans and trust products, private developers may also seek funding through bond issues in the form of Asset-Backed Securities (ABS). ABS are bonds backed by financial assets such as future income from the provision of infrastructure services from large-scale new developments. These financially engineered instruments carve out risks to match the risk appetite of a wider range of investors. As a result, the pricing of these bond tranches is likely to capture better pricing and may offer an attractive alternative for the distribution of financial risks associated with new city developments across domestic and international investors seeking those risks in China.

The Structural Mechanism of Financing New Cities in China

The total fixed asset invested in 131 state-level industrial parks in 2011 was RMB 2.09 trillion and accounted for 35% of the total national fixed asset investment (Shi 2013). Capital raised from *State Budget* accounted for 4.3% of the Total Investment in Fixed Assets in China,[20] whereas *Domestic Loans* and *Self-raised Funds* accounted for 13.4% and 66.3% accordingly (*Zhong Guo Tong Ji Nian Jian 2018* [*China Statistical Year Book 2018*] n.d.). State Budget includes revenues from National General Public Budget, National Government Funds (including Land Rent Revenue[21]), National State Capital Operations, National Social Insurance Funds, and Government Bonds.[22] In 2018 revenues from sale of land-use rights[23] accounted for 86.4% of National Government Funds revenue.

Domestic Loans includes loans made by domestic banks as well as national special loans.[24] For instance, bank loans borrowed by LGFVs are included within the *Domestic Loan* category ("Quan Guo Zheng Fu Xing Zhai Wu Shen Ji Jie Guo [Results Of The National Government Debt Audit]" 2013). Self-raised Funds refers to the funds raised by public or private enterprises and institutions. The major sources of the *Self-raised Funds* are LGFV Bonds and capitals raised through PPP projects.

As of mid-2013, 37.4% of the national government's debt was borrowed via LGFVs whereas 68% of the national government's debt was invested in municipal construction, land development, and transportation and infrastructure ("Quan Guo Zheng Fu Xing Zhai Wu Shen Ji Jie Guo [Results Of The National Government Debt Audit]" 2013).

---

19. Gu'an New Industry City is discussed in more depth in Chapter 6.
20. Total Investment in Fixed Assets in the Whole Country (China) refers to the volume of activities in construction and purchases of fixed assets (across China) and related fees. It includes fixed asset investments by type of ownership i.e. the investment by State-owned units, collective-owned units, joint ownership units, share-holding units, private units, individuals as well as investments by entrepreneurs from Hong Kong, Macao and Taiwan, foreign investors and others. See ("China Statistical Yearbook 2019" n.d.)
21. Land Rent includes Income from the transfer of state-owned land use rights, income from state-owned land income funds and income from agricultural land development funds.
22. Government bonds at all levels of governments, including local governments.
23. Also, sometimes referred to as: Land Rent Revenues
24. Domestic Loans refer to loans of various forms borrowed from banks and non-bank financial institutions for the purpose of investment in fixed assets. This includes loans issued by banks from their own funds and deposits, special loans by government (including loan for substituting petroleum with coal), loans arranged by local government from special funds, domestic reserve loans, and revolving loans, etc. See ("China Statistical Yearbook 2019" n.d.)

The Way Forward for Financing New Cities in China

According to Nobel Laureate Edmund Phelps, even though there have been periods in history when societies have experienced *dynamism* from the rapid growth and advances in technologies (in the authors' view urbanization would fall in the category of technological development), many societies have faltered moving beyond these periods of dynamism towards what he calls *vibrancy*. *Vibrancy* implies sustained dynamism as the benefits of the technological advancements become widespread and accrue for the benefit of the masses of citizens inhabiting those societies. These are periods of *mass flourishing* (Datta 2016). The second phase of China's urbanization could be considered as a period of *dynamism*.

Sustaining this dynamism and ensuring that its benefits will accrue to masses of urban citizens in existing and new cities across China, rather than be grandfathered to the benefit of a few advantaged ones, will be a challenge for future policy-making. The ability to choose from a wide range of market-based and innovative financing options is an integral element in the pursuit of this *urban vibrancy*. The new city financing challenges in China are both structural and incremental and therefore may offer rich potential for innovation in urban finance, with uniquely Chinese characteristics.

The pastures for theoretical and empirical engagement regarding future innovative financing mechanisms for new cities in China are abundant and may require a multifaceted exploration of some structural and administrative dimensions including but not limited to: (i) functionally aligning revenues and expenditures at the local vs. provincial vs. central administrative levels to mitigate the macro-economic distortions arising from the misalignment of incentives at local levels and excessive dependency on land-use monetization to meet social-infrastructure costs ("Urban China: Toward Efficient, Inclusive, and Sustainable Urbanization" n.d.); (ii) alignment of decision making related to funding fiscal gaps with the appropriate, functional, administrative level, while leaving some room for accommodation both at the local and central administrative levels; (iii) balancing the capital needed for future new city developments with access to a supply of capital from a diversity of sources so as to mitigate excessive, concentrated risk-taking by domestic savers, particularly vulnerable household segments; and (iv) enhancing the long-term efficiency of utilizing land as a source of developmental capital by reconfiguring developmental zoning and creating other novel forms of development rights to limit urban sprawl and thereby maintain a healthy supply of arable land to feed an increasing population.

China is often cited as a large economy with a *dwarf* currency. This is perhaps due to the excessively cautious approach of its policy makers towards full capital account convertibility. Building and expanding domestic municipal bond markets to encourage domestic and foreign investors offer an avenue for further expanding the acceptance of Renminbi in international financial markets. Increasingly funding domestic demand for financing new cities with ready-made sources of international capital could be done by issuing RMB denominated international bonds. They could be aimed at investors from trading-partner countries that enjoy a trade surplus with China, especially South Korea, Australia, Brazil, Switzerland, and Japan, and others. Structural financial sector reforms that facilitate a further reduction of the credit risk premium required by international investors from China's emerging debt markets, by encouraging an expansion of domestic municipal credit ratings agencies as well as facilitating a more open access to international rating agencies particularly from countries targeted for such investments, is another avenue that could be pursued.

As part of this evolution, increasingly adopting international standards for PPP projects to encourage the shift from land-based financing towards project-based financing and to encourage private sector participation in knowledge-accumulation through PPP projects in China are critical for the way forward. This could gradually reduce the substantial dependence on state-supported sources of debt financing of new cities, which poses substantial systemic risk (Zheng et al. 2017). A strategy that creates more market-based mechanisms and transitions towards greater equity and/ or equity-linked instruments for future urban financing would lead to better risk allocation and is likely to be essential to fulfilling China's aspirations of achieving sustainably vibrant new cities.

References

"2018 Nian Guo Min Jing Ji He She Hui Fa Zhan Tong Ji Gong Bao [2018 Statistical Communique On National Economic And Social Development]." 2019. February 28, 2019. http://www.stats.gov.cn/tjsj/zxfb/201902/t20190228_1651265.html.

Chang, C., and M. Lu. 2017. "Misery of New Town: Density, Distance and Debt." *Jingjixue Jikan (China Economic Quarterly)* 16 (4): 1621–42.

"Chapter 5 Local Government Bonds." 2019. In *The Future of China's Bond Market.* USA: INTERNATIONAL MONETARY FUND. https://www.elibrary.imf.org/view/IMF071/25402-9781484372142/25402-9781484372142/ch05.xml.

"China Statistical Yearbook 2019." n.d. Accessed February 7, 2020. http://www.stats.gov.cn/tjsj/ndsj/2019/indexeh.htm.

"China Statistical Yearbook-2014." n.d. Accessed November 1, 2019. http://www.stats.gov.cn/tjsj/ndsj/2014/indexee.htm.

Datta, Anusua. 2016. *Mass Flourishing—How Grassroots Innovation Created Jobs, Challenge and Change.* Springer.

Frey, David, Simon Gleave, Richard Dawson, J. Veihmeyer, A. Wang, J. Steward, and T. Lee & Wilschetz. 2014. "China's Urban Future: Financing a New Era of Urbanization." *KMPG International Cooperative*, no. 1.

"Guang Fa Hong Guan: Shen Me Shi Zhuan Xiang Zhai? [GF Securities: What Is Special Purpose Fund?]." 2018. 2018. https://finance.sina.com.cn/money/bond/research/2018-08-28/doc-ihikcahe8301714.shtml.

"Guo Wu Yuan Ban Gong Ting Guan Yu Gui Fan Guo You Tu Di Shi Yong Quan Chu Rang Shou Zhi Guan Li De Tong Zhi [Notice of the General Office of the State Council, PRC]." 2006. http://www.gov.cn/zwgk/2006-12/25/content_478251.html.

International Monetary Fund. Fiscal Affairs Dept. 2018. *Fiscal Monitor, April 2018 : Capitalizing on Good Times.* Fiscal Monitor.

"Quan Guo Zheng Fu Xing Zhai Wu Shen Ji Jie Guo [Results Of The National Government Debt Audit]." 2013. National Audit Office of the People's Republic of China. http://www.gov.cn/gzdt/2013-12/30/content_2557187.html.

Ren, Xuefei. 2013. *Urban China.* John Wiley & Sons.

Rithmire, Meg E. 2015. *Land Bargains and Chinese Capitalism: The Politics of Property Rights under Reform*. Cambridge University Press.

Shi, Rongyao. 2013. *Zhong Guo Kai Fa Qu Nian Jian 2012* [*Yearbook of China Development Zone 2012*)]. China Financial & Economic Publishing House.

"Urban China: Toward Efficient, Inclusive, and Sustainable Urbanization." n.d. World Bank. Accessed November 1, 2019. https://www.worldbank.org/en/country/china/publication/urban-china-toward-efficient-inclusive-sustainable-urbanization.

Zheng, Siqi, Zhan Shi, and Jing Wu. 2014. "Tu Di Chu Rang, Cheng Shi Jian She Yu Fang Di Chang Jia Ge - Dui Zhong Guo Te Se Cheng Shi Jian She Tou Rong Zi Mo Shi De Tan Tao [Land transfer, urban construction and real estate prices - Discussion on investment and financing mode of urban construction with Chinese characteristics]." *Academia Bimestrie*, no. 5: 157–163. https://doi.org/10.16091/j.cnki.cn32-1308/c.2014.05.058.

Zheng, Siqi, Weizeng Sun, Jianfeng Wu, and Matthew E. Kahn. 2017. "The Birth of Edge Cities in China: Measuring the Effects of Industrial Parks Policy." *Journal of Urban Economics* 100: 80–103.

Zhong Guo Tong Ji Nian Jian 2018 [*China Statistical Year Book 2018*]. n.d. China Statistics Press. Accessed December 7, 2019. http://www.stats.gov.cn/tjsj/ndsj/.

Chapter 5.

Digital Technology in Urban Systems: New Opportunities in New Cities

Zhengzhen Tan

To support vibrant economic activities, cities old and new depend on their *urban infrastructure systems* or *urban systems*—transportation, housing, office, retail, cultural amenities, green infrastructure, energy systems, water waste and etc. Economists have examined endowment of urban infrastructure is a key indicator of their economic performance.[1] Beijing's subway transit system affects local restaurant hours of operation, diversity, and consumer demand in the city's neighborhoods (Zheng et al. 2016). Modern urban economic theory and policymakers see the provision of consumer leisure amenities as a way to attract workers, especially the highly skilled and their employers. A study by Carlino and Saiz provides direct evidence of the importance of leisure amenities for economic growth of cities (Carlino and Saiz 2019).

Ever since the early days of human civilization, cities have depended on advances in the technology of urban systems to enable an economically, culturally, and socially vibrant place: that includes the electricity grid, street lighting, the subway system, smartphones as well as the cellular networks that power them. Each new generation of technologies empowers urban systems to meet cities' growing concentrations of people and activities. Cities are entering a stage of modern transformational change, in which they are shaped by technological innovation ("Report to the President: Technology and the Future of Cities" 2016). The stream of digital technologies bringing this transformational change includes geographic information systems (GIS), information and communication technology (ICT), the internet of things (IoT), data analytics, artificial intelligence (AI), machine learning, blockchain technology, mobile technologies, social media technologies, application programming interfaces (APIs), etc. Why is this stage of technological innovation transformational to urban growth? How do those technology investments contribute to economic vibrancy of cities?

Past studies show that communication technology has laid the foundation for economic growth benefitting cities large and small. Studies also show that digital technologies can have a profound impact on the prosperity of a region ("Smart Cities Council | Policy Frameworks and Tools" 2019). Smart city projects contribute to economic growth by establishing an economy of scale. The use of digital technology in the production of goods and services, in particular, has a strong influence on productivity and economic growth (Kramer, Jenkins, and Katz 2007). Research has suggested that the next generation of 5G wireless network infrastructure, for example, can transform local economies. With 5G, smart city solutions applied to managing vehicle traffic and electrical grids could produce USD $160 billion in benefits and

1. Kyu Sik Lee and Alex Anas demonstrate how companies locate in a city, and if they do not find the services they need, they invest in generating the services themselves (thereby exiting the system); or they apply pressure to obtain better services, with potential improvements in local governance; or they relocate to cities with better services (Anas and Lee 1996).

savings (Accenture Strategy 2017). While most of the current smart cities' projects are deployed in existing cities, by 2017 we see a new trend in the emerging new planned cities across world, i.e. Google's Toronto Waterfront or China's XiongAn. In those futuristic new cities, urban "digital layers" were designed, planned, and developed at the same time as the physical environment was developed.

Because of the short time horizon for building those digital new cities and the paucity of data and empirical information, this chapter is not an evaluation of the digital technology's impact on economic vibrancy. Instead it seeks to lay out a future research agenda about the ways in which transformational digital technologies contribute to the economic vibrancy of new cities and do so in different ways than traditional urban systems do. Although academia, industry, and city leaders like to claim that new technologies will transform their new city planning, design, construction, and operation in revolutionary ways, validating or disproving such claims will require decades of development. Such is the case of Zhengdong New District and GuAn New District, for example. This chapter, therefore, presents a hypothetical framework on how digital innovation is transforming traditional urban systems by creating digital urban systems, which are more efficient and human-centered and thereby increase the economic vibrancy of the new city. In the case of XiongAn new city, although its urban economic vibrancy cannot be established because it's still in the early planning stage, I examine how the city administration approaches its digital city system in alignment with its physical planning and industry development strategies—not simply as the deployment of new technologies but also by designing its institutional governance, data framework, and innovation ecosystem. I hypothesize that this new generation of new planned city-making will be transformed by digital technology and demonstrates the potential to achieve greater and faster vibrancy in the years to come.

Digital Urban Systems

Before the digital age, traditional urban systems included a physical, infrastructural layer and a human service layer. A traditional urban public transportation system, for example, comprised a physical infrastructural layer (roads, tunnels, etc.) and a service layer, (bus service, traffic light service, subway service, etc.). The main difference between traditional urban systems and digital urban systems is that the latter introduces a third layer in between the physical and service layers: a digital (or data) layer.

In a traditional economy, urban systems play an "enabling" role in urban development: Transportation, energy, housing, and amenity systems enable cities to agglomerate economic activities and create a vibrant economy. Adding and integrating the digital layer between the physical and service layers usually takes place in three phases: digitizing the urban system, digitalizing the urban system and, finally, digitally transforming the urban system.[2] Digitization refers to taking analog information and encoding it so that computers can store, process, and transmit that information. Converting the handwritten text of a bus schedule into the digital information that appears on a website or app is an example of digitization. Digitalization means improving the urban system's efficiencies by using digitized information. Digitalization indicates more penetrating transformations of traditional infrastructures into informational systems capable of dynamically mediating interactions among residents and businesses in their urban contexts. Moreover, digitalization increases the possibilities of improving the operational efficiencies of urban systems. In case of a digitalized public transportation system, bus data optimizes bus routes as well as schedule planning. Other operations can also be automated. A single transportation card—an Octopus card in Hong Kong or a T-Money card in Seoul, for example—can be used on all modes of public transportation, and information about different modes of transportation is consolidated for riders on apps or public display screens. And decision-makers are indeed relying more and more on the value of data to make key decisions for their transport networks.

Digitization and digitalization enable cities to become more connected and enable data-driven operation. Digital transformation is the process of devising new service applications that integrate all of this data and digitalized applications. Data is easily accessible for use across various platforms, devices, interfaces. As Singapore is striving towards a car-lite society, with the development of smart mobility technology, Singapore has more progressive digital visions of "mobility as a service."[3] Thanks to digitalized public transformation systems citizens will ultimately be able to subscribe to "mobility packages" and to use public transportation, car-sharing services, rentals, and so on in a seamless manner ("Smart Nation Initiatives | Singapore's Efforts to Improve Living" n.d.). Designing digital urban systems this way offers new business models and put users at the center of its operation.

Digitization, digitalization and digital transformation are terms that are often used indistinguishably. Although they are appropriately associated with smart cities,[4] the academic community still suffers from lack of agreement about the definition of a smart city (Hollands 2008). The term "smart cities" started as a marketing label widely adopted by ICT corporations and cities alike. First generation smart city projects feature digitization of urban system using information communications technology (ICTs). Big ICT multinational enterprises such as IBM and Cisco provided

---

2. Refer to Gartner Glossary, Information Technology ("Digitization" n.d.).
3. Mobility as a Service (MaaS), defined by Deloitte as a data-driven, customer-centric paradigm powered by the pervasiveness of smartphones.
4. When one considers that 'digital transformation' once referred to 'digitization' and 'digitalization' was once called 'Informationization'. Therefore, for our analysis, we will use the term, digitization, digitalization and digital, while smart cities sometimes refer to either or all of the terms.

the digitized infrastructures to tackle the data-driven, operational challenges of cities. Smart cities can therefore refer to any of the three processes identified above. Digitization and digitalization of urban systems are often top-down, project-driven initiatives. During those two processes, digital technologies are deployed as engineering projects as is evident throughout first-generation, Asian, smart-city initiatives in which cities purchased digitally enhanced, single-purpose solutions that reflected a twentieth-century, monofunctional, infrastructural design mentality.

Digital Cities and Their Impact on Economic Development

Cities have always been important engines of economic growth. They are assuming an even greater importance in today's knowledge-driven, innovation economy, especially where place-based ecosystems are critical to economic growth. Cities benefit from attracting and retaining knowledge-workers or companies looking for a place to settle or to visit. As cities compete, every city-based service can be decisive. China has transitioned from a manufacturing-based economy to a service-based economy. In 2015 China's service sector reached 50% of its total GDP.[5] In the New Economy structure, greater value is created from an economy of services than from the manufacturing sector or the agricultural sector; wealth is created more through using human knowledge and creativity than through extracting and processing of natural resources (Bank 2007). In contrast, twenty-first-century industries will depend on generating knowledge through creativity and innovation (Landry and Bianchini 1995). According to Hospers, the knowledge economy and globalization has led to the point where cities have to compete for the favors of residents, companies, and visitors (Hospers 2003).

Furthermore, cities are not just containers for people and business, their urban systems enables connections to take place, networks to be built, and innovative combinations to be consummated (Florida, Adler, and Mellander 2017). Jacobs famously theorized that prevailing theories of innovation and economic development going back to Adam Smith emphasize efficiency and the division of labor but fail to account for the key inputs that drive innovation. Those, she argued, were less a product of firms and more a product of cities that bring together the diversity of economic assets and actors required for innovative and entrepreneurial activity (Jacobs 2016). In a knowledge-based economy, cities become the key unit of innovation, creativity, and economy growth. Urban systems enable and foster the

5. It was 50.2% ("China Statistical Yearbook-2015" n.d.), and in 2012 it was the first time that service sector catches up with the secondary industry (45.3% vs 45.3%)

combination and recombination of knowledge and creativities, and therefore play a more and more critical role in economic development than in a manufacturing economy.

To examine how digital urban system can potentially enhance economic development, I will describe my hypothesis from two perspectives that lead to transformational changes in digital urban systems. On one hand digital urban systems improve operational efficiency: A digitalized urban system enables new operations models that help unlock the economic value of place-based resources (Li et al. 2016); on the other hand, they improve user experience and facilitate human-centric strategic transformation. Digital urban systems offer opportunities for public and private organizations to design and deliver customer-centric services.

Firstly, digital urban systems improve operation efficiency. City service providers build on and leverage a digital layer to connect physical goods, services, and people with real-time data driven processes, in online-to-offline operations. Most recent Chinese smart cities applications focus on civic services, transportation, public safety, energy, and environment, public health, smart water and sewage infrastructure, etc. Digital technologies make the connections tighter, faster, more personal, and more comprehensive between service providers and users. Sharing-economy business models are emerging that enable more efficient use of physical assets, such as cars or real estate, and provide new sources of income to city residents. The private sector can make profitable services such as bicycle sharing, intelligent trash bins, and smart street sweeping, to name a few. As Richard Florida observes: from food delivery start-ups to mapping and co-living companies, technology focused on urban systems is drawing billions of dollars in venture capital ("'Urban Tech' Is Unleashing Creative Destruction on Cities - CityLab"). In May 2018, Softbank China led the USD 21 million Series B financing of CowaRobot. The autonomous ground sweeping sanitation robots by CowaRobot would be used in Changsha, Shanghai, Wuhu, Hefei, Guangzhou, and many other Chinese cities. The street sanitation services, traditionally operated by the street sanitation unit, are being commercialized. Another example of how emergent digital city start-ups are changing the operation models of urban infrastructure and services reflects one of the biggest problems facing many Chinese cities: there is a severe shortage of parking spaces, estimated at 60 million too few. Governments, local and national alike, are incentivizing the private investment of smart parking facilities, with the government procuring their operational services. Smart vertical parking, shared parking, and curbside parking have generated tremendous entrepreneurial and investment activities. In 2005 there were over 200 start-ups in the smart parking industry. Leading companies like ETPC, TJD Parking, AI Park have attracted billions of dollars investment from venture capitalists.

Secondly, increasing numbers of new services and economic activities in digital urban systems enhance economic vibrancy, thereby improving the experiences of residents and businesses. China's cities and other Asian cities have accelerated the development of digital urban systems to improve the experiences of their inhabitants and to address environmental sustainability, urban resilience, and resource efficiency issues. At around the same time that China launched its 200 smart cities projects in 2010, China's urbanization was reaching a turning point. Under the new paradigm of "National New-Type Urbanization ("Guo Jia Xin Xing Cheng Zhen Hua Gui Hua (2014 - 2020 Nian) [The National New-Type Urbanization Plan (2014-2020)]" n.d.)," all levels of government aim today to transform China's urbanization from a top-down, physical-infrastructure-driven mode of development to a human-centric and service-driven mode to address poor user experience caused by urbanization pressures.

Digital technology innovations are opening up new opportunities to develop governance approaches that enable citizen-driven urban governance models. The Third Plenary Session of the 18th Central Committee of the Communist Party of China took place in November 2013. For the first time, it raised the notion of "modern governance system" and "modern governance capability." The National New-Type Urbanization Plan (2014-2020) ("Guo Jia Xin Xing Cheng Zhen Hua Gui Hua (2014 - 2020 Nian) [The National New-Type Urbanization Plan (2014-2020)]" n.d.) states that "based on a human-centered, service-led principal, cities should improve their urban governance structure, innovate urban governance approaches, and upgrade urban societal governance capacities." Since then, a handful of other state council working meetings and policies have shifted the paradigm of top-down, urban management (Guan Li) to bilateral urban governance (Zhi Li). Citizens are empowered to participate in the urban system management processes thanks to the prevalence of real-time communication and opinion-sharing channels. Through an app called Jia Zhu Jia Men (home in Xiamen), for example, a digital community governance platform start-up helps to process citizen's voices and opinions as continuous input into the decision-making processes; their involvement monitors public administrations initiatives in real time and increases pressure on the decision-makers to hold them accountable. This type of system is shaping new rules for the governance of urban system.

Towards Digital City Vision: XiongAn New District

In 2017 two new planned cities, one in Canada and one in China, caught the attention of city governments, urbanists, and industry leaders across the globe: Google's Toronto Waterfront and China's XiongAn New Distric. Waterfront Toronto and Google's Sidewalk Lab announced their ambitious new plan for their Toronto waterfront development, located southeast of downtown Toronto. According to Canada's Prime Minister Justin Trudeau, Sidewalk Labs would create a testbed for new technologies that would help to build smarter, greener, more inclusive cities, which they hope to see scale across Toronto's Eastern Waterfront and eventually around the world. The scale of Sidewalk Toronto's planning area is only around 3 square kilometers, that is one thirtieth of the size of XiongAn first phase plan: the planned area of XiongAn New District is 2000 square kilometers, with 100 square kilometers as its first phase. The planned population of XiongAn is 6 million in 20 years, whereas Toronto Waterfront is dramatically less. Toronto Waterfront and XiongAn represent the two most high-profile new planned cities where digital technology is shaping the physical and industrial planning, development, and operations. The plan is to integrate digital urban systems in the physical city and industry planning in the full lifecycle of city development: planning, construction, operations, and governance ("Xiong An Shu Zi Cheng Shi - Zhong Guo Xiong An Ji Tuan [XiongAn Digital City - China XiongAn Group]" n.d.). In the XiongAn New District case study described below, we examine the new city's holistic approach to designing a digital city vision in which digital technologies change how the city goes about defining its urban infrastructure systems and competitive strategy.

On April 1, 2017, China announced plans to establish the XiongAn New District (XiongAn hereafter), about 100 km southwest of Beijing. Known as China's "city of the future," XiongAn was designed to become a zone for innovation, a digital city synchronized with a brick-and-mortar one, and a livable and business-friendly area. The state-owned Assets Supervision and Administration Commission of the State Council announced it would encourage state firms to support development of the area. Telecom giants China Mobile and China Telecom declared that they would make sure XiongAn was covered by a 5G network ahead of many other places in the country. China Development Bank, a state-owned policy bank, said it would soon provide loans of RMB 130 billion (USD 18.9 billion) to support XiongAn's development. The digital city planning of XiongAn New District was conducted as joint effort of the XiongAn New District Government's Reform and Development Bureau and China Electronics Technology Group Company (CETC)'s smart city arm, The New Smart City Research Institute of China Electronics Technology Group Company.

The physical planning guideline[6], the digital infrastructure guidelines, and the industry development policy were planned simultaneously. According to the XiongAn's *Planning Guideline*, there will be convergence of transformations in urbanization, digitalization, and industrialization. It demonstrates a digital city vision, in which urban systems are not based on a single-system framework as seen in the architectural design of most smart cities; instead it is fully integrated into the physical planning. If digitization and digitalization are about technology engineering, digital transformation requires cities to deal better with change

6. XiongAn's physical planning guideline was approved by State Council in April 2018 ("He Bei Xiong An Xin Qu Gui Hua Gang Yao [Hebei XiongAn's Physical Planning Guideline]" 2018).

overall, and to realize their human-centered vision for society, including values such as livability, sustainability, and justice. A user-centric, strategic transformation requires city administration's organizational change as well as the implementation of digital technologies. For example, if technological advances are not accompanied by institutional innovations, this can result in an incoherence between institutions and technologies in urban infrastructure systems, which can in turn have a negative impact on the performance of cities (Razaghi and Finger 2018).

In this regard, new planned cities like XiongAn provide a good opportunity and a blank slate for the digital transformation of urban systems with holistic designs in all aspects of city-making. As India's state official Amitabh Kant, CEO of the National Institution for Transforming India and former CEO of the Delhi Mumbai Industrial Corridor Development Corporation, has stated, in much of the developed world, innovative new digital technologies are being retrofitted onto aging infrastructure to make cities work better for the 21st century. But here in India we have a tremendous opportunity: to build new cities from the ground up with smart technologies" (Datta 2015).

In addition to technological advancement, how does XiongAn New Cities planning and development differ from a traditional new planned city where digital layer is more of an afterthought? The XiongAn new district embodies a new approach towards a digital city vision of institutions, data frameworks, and the innovation ecosystem.

Institutional Organization.

Traditionally, a functional understanding of urban infrastructures leads to the dominance of siloed organizational structures to manage them. This is reflected in a typical organizational structure in city administrations with separate departments in charge of transportation, water, energy, and housing services. The divisions in charge of these functions are usually managing their own areas of concern in an almost independent manner from one another. The corresponding administrative entities become very technical and narrowly focused on solving their own problems, seldom feeling an urgency to communicate with each other. While a typical city administration usually consists of different bureaus to operate and govern urban infrastructural systems, the XiongAn Administration Committee (Guan Wei Hui) organizes all urban systems administration department (i.e. transportation, housing, energy, water& sewage, waste under one Bureau of Public Service. The Public Service Bureau aims to break functional solos and integrate the planning, construction, and governance of different infrastructure departments to enable a user-centric approach to city services.

Data Frameworks and Infrastructure.

The Block Data Platform ("Kuai Shu Ju Ping Tai Lai Le [The Block Data Platform Is Coming]" n.d.) is XiongAn administration's initiative to centrally coordinate data to facilitate cross-functional digital services to its citizen. Using the Block Data Platform, the CETC team is working on building digital services from the community level up. A coordinated data strategy and framework platform is the foundation for developing a sustainable business model and operation model for urban services: 1) governance services; 2) public services; 3) facility management services; and 4) commercial services. A sustainable business model and the various services can be inspiring to its citizens and businesses. Legal frameworks and infrastructure for open data enable integrated customer-centric service innovation. Unlike traditional urban systems, which are operated and governed in isolation, digital urban systems grow in value by working with other systems. The value captured from data-driven digital infrastructures typically dramatically expands when it is networked with other data (Alvarez 2017). Therefore, a coordinated data strategy is needed. To accelerate a future for integrated urban systems, XiongAn administration is building platform and infrastructure on the interconnections between systems and sectors. One example is intelligent light pole. The Intelligent Light pole will integrate the systems of lighting, traffic monitoring, public safety monitoring, pollution and air quality monitoring, Wifi/5G network, broadcasting, info display, charging station.

Actively Building an Innovation Ecosystem in a Digital City.

Technology conglomerates such as China Mobile launched the Urban Innovation Challenges in May 2019 to solicit smart city innovation project proposals that apply 5G. One of China's leading tech incubators and investment funds company, Tustar, set up the "XiongAn Tustar International Innovation Center." Innovation ecosystems enable collaboration among key stakeholders, i.e. government, startups, industries leaders, universities/NGOs, and risk capital investors. This makes it easier to unlock the economic value of urban services.

Future Research Agenda

Compared to digital transformation of existing cities, new planned digital cities may provide a faster or more sustainable way to achieve economic vibrancy. Unlike most existing cities smart city projects that are deployed at municipal or district level, XiongAn built its digital infrastructure from the community level up to enable various residents' daily services. With a sustainable business model focused on users' service application will bring an integrated user experience of urban systems and foster vibrancy. Further studies and fieldwork will be needed to examine the impact of digital urban systems on achieving economic vibrancy as XiongAn's development evolves. Future research will be needed in the XiongAn case to validate my hypothesis regarding the relationship between digital urban system and economic vibrancy: it will be necessary to review the GDP, the creation of firms and jobs, and measure consumption. Further studies will also need to examine critical digital infrastructure, i.e. transportation, street light, housing, energy & environment amenities, to measure how they enhance urban economic vibrancy.

References

Accenture Strategy. 2017. "How 5G Can Help Municipalities Become Vibrant Smart Cities."

Alvarez, Ricardo. 2017. "The Relevance of Informational Infrastructures in Future Cities." *Field Actions Science Reports. The Journal of Field Actions*, no. Special Issue 17: 12–15.

Anas, Alex, and Kyu Sik Lee. 1996. "The Benefits of Alternative Power Tariffs for Nigeria and Indonesia." SSRN Scholarly Paper ID 636132. Rochester, NY: Social Science Research Network. https://papers.ssrn.com/abstract=636132.

Asian Development Bank. 2007. *Moving Towards Knowledge-Based Economies: Asian Experiences*. Asian Development Bank. https://www.adb.org/publications/moving-towards-knowledge-based-economies-asian-experiences.

Carlino, Gerald A., and Albert Saiz. 2019. "Beautiful City: Leisure Amenities and Urban Growth." *Journal of Regional Science* 59 (3): 369–408.

"China Statistical Yearbook-2015." n.d. Accessed February 10, 2020. http://www.stats.gov.cn/tjsj/ndsj/2015/indexeh.htm.

Datta, Ayona. 2015. "New Urban Utopias of Postcolonial India: 'Entrepreneurial Urbanization'in Dholera Smart City, Gujarat." *Dialogues in Human Geography* 5 (1): 3–22.

"Digitization." n.d. Gartner. Accessed February 10, 2020. https://www.gartner.com/en/information-technology/glossary/digitization.

Florida, Richard, Patrick Adler, and Charlotta Mellander. 2017. "The City as Innovation Machine." *Regional Studies* 51 (1): 86–96.

"Guo Jia Xin Xing Cheng Zhen Hua Gui Hua (2014 - 2020 Nian) [The National New-Type Urbanization Plan (2014-2020)]." n.d. Accessed February 5, 2020. http://www.gov.cn/zhengce/2014-03/16/content_2640075.htm.

"He Bei Xiong An Xin Qu Gui Hua Gang Yao [Hebei XiongAn's Physical Planning Guideline]." 2018. Sina. 2018. https://finance.sina.com.cn/china/2018-04-21/doc-ifznefkh3271111.shtml.

Hollands, Robert G. 2008. "Will the Real Smart City Please Stand up? Intelligent, Progressive or Entrepreneurial?" *City* 12 (3): 303–320.

Hospers, Gert-Jan. 2003. "Creative Cities: Breeding Places in the Knowledge Economy." *Knowledge, Technology & Policy* 16 (3): 143–162.

Jacobs, Jane. 2016. *The Death and Life of Great American Cities*. Vintage.

Kramer, William J., Beth Jenkins, and Robert S. Katz. 2007. "The Role of the Information and Communications Technology Sector in Expanding Economic Opportunity." *Cambridge, MA: Kennedy School of Government, Harvard University*.

"Kuai Shu Ju Ping Tai Lai Le [The Block Data Platform Is Coming]." n.d. Accessed February 5, 2020. http://m.news.cctv.com/2019/11/20/ARTIC9KoqUHjFBXbNfn5bFjJ191120.shtml.

Landry, Charles, and Franco Bianchini. 1995. "The Creative City Demos." *Comedia, London*.

Li, Feng, Alberto Nucciarelli, Sinead Roden, and Gary Graham. 2016. "How Smart Cities Transform Operations Models: A New Research Agenda for Operations Management in the Digital Economy." *Production Planning & Control* 27 (6): 514–528.

Razaghi, Mohamad, and Matthias Finger. 2018. "Smart Governance for Smart Cities." *Proceedings of the IEEE* 106 (4): 680–689.

"Report to the President: Technology and the Future of Cities." 2016. https://www.whitehouse.gov/sites/whitehouse.gov/files/images/Blog/PCAST%20Cities%20Report%20_%20FINAL.pdf.

"Smart Cities Council | Policy Frameworks and Tools." 2019. August 12, 2019. https://smartcitiescouncil.com/taxonomy/term/562.

"Smart Nation Initiatives | Singapore's Efforts to Improve Living." n.d. Accessed February 5, 2020. http://www.smartnation.sg/what-is-smart-nation/initiatives/Transport.

"'Urban Tech' Is Unleashing Creative Destruction on Cities - CityLab." n.d. Accessed February 5, 2020. https://www.citylab.com/life/2018/07/the-rise-of-urban-tech/564653/.

"Xiong An Shu Zi Cheng Shi - Zhong Guo Xiong An Ji Tuan [XiongAn Digital City - China XiongAn Group]." n.d. Accessed February 5, 2020. http://www.chinaxiongan.cn/GB/419268/419275/index.html.

Zheng, Siqi, Xiaoke Hu, Jianghao Wang, and Rui Wang. 2016. "Subways near the Subway: Rail Transit and Neighborhood Catering Businesses in Beijing." *Transport Policy* 51: 81–92.

Chapter 6.

Zhengdong: the "Metabolic" and "Eco-Smart" Approaches to Long-Term Vibrancy[1]

Colleen Chiu-Shee, Ningdi Wei, Siqi Zheng

In human history, societies have developed in concert with attempts to build new cities. But today the scale of new plans and speed of building new cities are unprecedented. Having established more than 600 new cities since 1949, China is regarded as the global epicenter for new city building (Shepard 2015). Most of them are still under development. Lessons for building new cities are widely sought-after. Zhengdong New District (Figure 6.1), once considered a ghost city, has risen in economic vibrancy in recent years (Ye 2019). It is now regarded as one of China's most advanced and economically successful new cities and a paradigm for China's New-Type Urbanization (Cai 2019; Xinhuanet n.d.). As more new cities await future development, a reflection on Zhengdong's experience is particularly timely and meaningful for city-making attempts elsewhere—both within and beyond China.

As one of the pioneers in China's new cities movement, Zhengdong New District is proud of its increasing economic competitiveness, vibrant public spaces, agreeable environment, and enhanced quality of life (Zi 2012). Zhengdong is one of China's first new cities planned with comprehensive urban functions. It is also a pioneering new city that has incorporated ideologies of internationally renowned designers. Since its conception, Zhengdong has consistently received political support from the top. Zhengdong's initiators include Li Keqiang, who has risen to be China's premier and continues emphasizing Zhengdong's development. Aiming at high standards for development, local authorities have always searched for and experimented with the most innovative design and planning ideas, such as "eco" and "smart" approaches. Yet, implementing internationally advanced approaches in local contexts demands tremendous trial and error and consistent efforts of administrative coordination and local management.

Tapping into Zhengdong's unique experience, we seek to uncover the key strategies of its planning and development that have laid a foundation for its current vibrancy. Central China, where Zhengdong is located, was once a region with low economic competitiveness and was losing population to Coastal China. Zhengdong's development has gained the reputation as a success, leading the rise of Central China. It showcases what Chinese governments can achieve in building an astonishing new city from scratch.

This chapter looks at Zhengdong's development strategies and addresses three questions: 1) How was Zhengdong's masterplan conceived? 2) How vibrant is Zhengdong's economy and what are some financing and development strategies? and 3) How is Zhengdong preparing for future development? The chapter highlights the

---

1. The research is supported by the Sustainable Urbanization Lab at Massachusetts Institute of Technology and the Administrative Committee of Zhengdong New District. We thank Zhengzhou's municipal government and local planners and developers for sharing their knowledge and providing data. We also thank Dongxiao Niu's excellent research assistance.

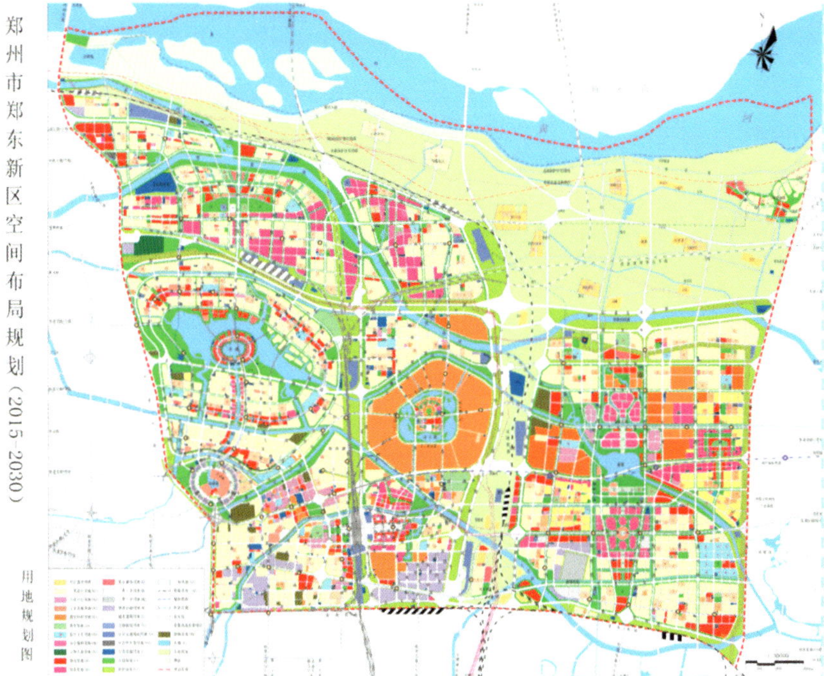

Figure 6.1: Zhengdong New District Locator Map.
Source: Administrative Committee of Zhengdong New District

Figure 6.2: The Masterplan of Zhengdong New District designed by Kisho Kurokawa and Associates.
Source: Administrative Committee of Zhengdong New District

promoted ideal of the city, exhibits some observable qualities of the city, and parses the rationales underlying the new city's conception and implementation strategy. Examining Zhengdong's development eighteen years after its inception, this chapter is one of the first attempts to assess Zhengdong's strategies for overall planning and design, economic development, urban management and future transitions in a retrospective manner. The discussion on Zhengdong sheds light on the impact of a state-led, holistically planned new city in developing contexts and invites future research about potential approaches to creating vibrant new cities.

The Conception of Zhengdong New District

The City of Zhengzhou is located in Central China, a region that has large rural populations and that has been losing its populations to coastal provinces.[2] Compared with more developed regions in China, provinces in Central China are largely perceived by citizens and investors to be underdeveloped, lacking attractive characteristics in their urban and natural environment, and growing at a slack pace. Henan province is one such example. By the turn of the twenty-first century, China's central government had recognized the regional imbalance of development and has been searching for strategies to spur growth in central provinces. Henan province pioneered the rise of Central China, and Zhengdong was chosen by its government officials to showcase Henan's promising future (Governa and Sampieri 2019). The conception of Zhengdong New District took place against the backdrop of growth ambitions in Central China.

Around the year 2000, the City of Zhengzhou saw its need for urban expansion and decided to relocate a military airport which was sitting right outside the city's east border. The relocation vacated a plot of developable land, which seeded the city's plan to expand eastward. Expanding Henan's capital city also aligned with the province's political goal to gain regional competitiveness. At that time, Henan was a province with a low rate of urbanization. Its economy relied largely on agriculture, heavy industries, and low-end manufacturing. Central China's population was leaving for top-tier cities and coastal provinces. Henan's officials believed that Zhengzhou, as the capital city, bore the mission to spur provincial growth. Henan's officials aspired to build Zhengzhou into a vibrant economic center in Central China and planned to heighten its urban growth. Yet, the region lacked sophisticated development institutions, and Zhengdong's existing urbanization largely occurred in a piecemeal,

2. According to The Rise of Central China plan (zhong bu jue qi ji hua), announced by the then Premier Wen Jiabao in 2004, the central region includes six provinces: Shanxi, Henan, Anhui, Hubei, Hunan and Jiangxi.

uncoordinated manner. The provincial and municipal governments saw the necessity to create an effective growth plan in order to avoid disordered expansion, foster advanced, non-polluting industries, and, more importantly, to showcase Henan's potential to be an economically vibrant and livable region. They imbued tremendous ambitions in Zhengdong New District and envisioned it as a paradigm of city-making, which would showcase Henan's and Zhengzhou's capabilities for creating economic vibrancy.

With strong political support from Henan's then provincial governor Li Keqiang and its then mayor Li Ke, an ambitious expansion plan emerged shortly after 2000. The plan was to develop an additional area of 150 square kilometers right outside Zhengzhou's east urban border. The planned new area was 18 square kilometers larger than the city's total urban area at that time and was located on rural land. In 2001 Zhengzhou announced an international design competition and invited six globally renowned design firms to generate a schematic master plan for Zhengdong New District. The six firms included Kisho Kurokawa and Associates from Japan, Cox from Australia, Sasaki Associates from the United States, Arte Jean Marie Charpentier & Associates from France, PED Consultants from Singapore and the China Urban Planning Institute from Beijing. In order to decide on a winning scheme, local authorities organized expert reviews and public voting to solicit experts' and citizens' opinions. Local officials remark that the masterplan by Kisho Kurokawa and his associates incorporated both modern ideologies and design approaches from the developed world as well as cultural elements and philosophies originating in East Asia. Today, Kurokawa's plan is branded as the winner thanks to selections made by both local authorities and the public.[3]

Zhengzhou's plan to build a new area that was larger than its existing urban area was regarded as a bold move. The city's officials wondered whether building such a new city from scratch could ever be achievable.[4] Several planners and scholars warned against the high economic and environmental costs of building the new city and considered the plan to be impractical. Yet, Henan's provincial government projected massive urbanization in the following decade. To them, building new cities was inevitable. They resolved to fully implement Kurokawa's masterplan.

In order to realize Kurokawa's masterplan, Zhengdong planned to construct vast manmade lakes, a network of new ecologies, and extensive infrastructures—all completely from scratch on a massive scale within three to five years. For example, Longhu Lake was proposed to be as large as West Lake in Hangzhou, in Zhejiang

3. Some interviewees argue anecdotally that Kurokawa's plan was chosen mainly due to officials' preference, whereas the public voting was more for formality.
4. Information provided by officials who participated in the conception of Zhengdong during interviews.

province, southeast of Zhengdong. This bold plan garnered skepticism and received criticism from many urban experts, especially at planning review meetings and an annual meeting of China's planning association. The bone of contention was the feasibility of constructing large-scale lakes in a water-scarce city like Zhengzhou. The original plan proposed channeling water from the Yellow River into the new lakes. Zhengzhou and other cities nearby, however, all relied on water from the Yellow River to provide drinking water. According to China's policy, the City of Zhengzhou had a limited quota for its annual volume of water channeling. Experts questioned whether Zhengzhou would have enough water to fill the new lakes. Zhengzhou's government eventually resolved the water shortage issue with the development of China's South-to-North Water Diversion Project—one of China's most expensive engineering projects in history—which increasingly provided drinking water to cities innorthern China. Today, all of Zhengzhou's drinking water comes from the Project. The usage of water from the Yellow River that was originally allowed has been repurposed for landscaping. Local officials celebrate solving their water resource problem thanks to China's high-profile engineering project.

According to the original designers of Zhengdong New District, Kurokawa had integrated design principles that derive from the five forms of an ideal city into Zhengdong's blueprint. These ideal cities include a symbiotic city, a circular city, a metabolic city, an eco-city, and a regional-cultural city. In his vision, the new city would grow in clusters, all connected by infrastructural superstructures. Each cluster would have a particular functional focus, supported by associated industries, amenities, and services. The scale of each cluster was determined based on considerations to facilitate human-oriented activities as opposed to vehicular mobility. The combination of each cluster's programs would allow for self-sufficient urban systems within the new area and hence ensure its overall economic vibrancy. Such cluster-based growth processes were inspired by how biological cells grow in living bodies. Accordingly, multiple clusters would form symbiotic relationships, supporting each other's performance and collectively shaping a holistic city that could fully support all dimensions of working and living.

In the meantime Zhengdong would remain an element of Zhengzhou overall and form a symbiotic relationship with the old urban area. The origin of Zhengdong's underlying design thinking can be traced back to the architectural movement during Japan's post-WWII years, called Metabolism (*shinchintaisha*), which was introduced to the world in the 1950s by a group of young, progressive-minded Japanese architects, the Metabolists. The Metabolist utopias of modern Japan fused ideas about architectural megastructures with those of organic biological growth (Lin 2010). The organization of Metabolist cities featured multiscalar, symbiotic linkages among multiple elements of the city and between each element and the whole, with the linkages supported by connective, enabling superstructures. Kurokawa's teacher Kenzo Tange had largely influenced the Metabolists and remained a mentor for them. Zhengdong's designers believe that its scheme presents similar features of superstructures and clusters that are evident in Tange's plan for Tokyo Bay Area.

Designers of Zhengdong also argue that Kurokawa's scheme was influenced by the eco-city paradigm that emerged in the 1970s. Kurokawa envisioned a symbiotic relationship between nature and the city. The superstructures of the new city included not only new transportation and technological infrastructures but also newly constructed ecosystems and landscapes. The latter would allow for the co-flourishing of diverse ecological and socio-cultural activities, building an agreeable environment, encouraging healthy lifestyles, and enhancing urban dwellers' happiness. As an architect who was greatly influenced by Modernistic ideals, Kurokawa adopted a salient, geometric logic for Zhengdong's master layout. Zhengdong's Central Business District (CBD) presents a concentric composition. The center of the CBD is a circular, manmade lake surrounded by civic complexes—such as the exhibition and concert halls. Parks, transit lines, major roads, recreational paths, greenbelts, buildings of financial institutions, commercial-residential complexes—all surround a central lake,Ruyi Lake, in the form of concentric rings, connected by roads and green areas radiating from the center. Kurokawa believed that the circular city was an efficient model that could bring multiple benefits to the city: a concentric layout could ensure the legibility of the urban pattern, enhance the efficiency of flows, shape an iconic appearance, establish a strong identity for the city, and provide its residents with pride and a sense of belonging.

The provincial and municipal officials found the rationales underlying Kurokawa's long-term plan for growing a new city to be highly sensible and expressed great respect to this internationally renowned star architect. They were committed to almost fully adopting Kurokawa's plan and were determined to realize the entire scheme as it was proposed. Consistent implementation of massive urban developments had always been a challenge in practice, especially with China's frequent leadership changes and volatile policy adjustments. In order to prevent current and future officials from altering the original plan, in February 2002 Zhengzhou's municipal government pushed a bill through Zhengzhou's People's Congress that established Zhengdong's masterplan as a local regulation in order to warrant the faithful implementation of the original masterplan by all authorities, including those who were yet to be appointed. The city also assembled Zhengdong's Administrative Committee (ZAC) to coordinate and carry out the new city's development and subsequent management. In January 2003 the construction of the exhibition center broke ground, marking the start of the construction of the entire Zhengdong New District. To ensure both the quality and efficiency of its implementation, officials advocated using two slogans: one called for "high-standard planning and high-quality construction"; the other set three implementation milestones for the following decade—"to shape the iconic core area in three years, to lay all the foundational infrastructures in five years, and to construct the entire planned area by the end of the tenth year." The speed and sequence of urban construction highlighted by Zhengdong largely exemplify China's most common approach to building cities.

Building the core area of the CBD and its surrounding infrastructures and landscapes was crucial to kick off the entire new area and establish the city's new identity. The CBD was the initial demonstration of Zhengdong's potential to become a vibrant new city and of the capabilities of its authorities. The initial constructions included building the exhibition hall and its surrounding high-rises, excavating the lakes and connective canals, and constructing several large urban parks and wetlands. Concomitant with the construction of the starting zone were village clearance, resettlement projects, and major roads construction. These large-scale civic projects required a tremendous investment of public funds, with additional support from state-owned enterprises (SOEs) and land-based financing.

The start of the ambitious new city was fraught with tensions. Its initial constructions faced temporary financial difficulties and was contested for its massive alteration of the original human settlements, farmland, and ecosystems. Even after five years of development, the new city was still regarded as a ghost city, but the initial development laid solid groundwork for Zhengdong's subsequent growth. Its development took flight around 2008, when investments from major developers surged. While local real estate companies remained wary of investing in this new area, developers who had made a great fortune from investing in top-tier and coastal cities foresaw Zhengdong's potential and competed to claim their ground in the CBD and near the new high-speed railway station. At the meantime, municipal authorities designated Zhengdong to be the location for all new developments, especially high-rises. Provincial authorities also incentivized major financial institutions, large SOEs, and several universities to relocate their main headquarters and campuses to Zhengdong in clusters with corresponding functions. By 2010, the occupancy rate of the CBD had reached 90 percent. By 2013, the area had a population of 1.03 million residents. Its land sales prices became the highest in the City of Zhengzhou. Its housing prices increased 62.3 percent in 2014. Today, Zhengdong New District includes over 226 national and international financial institutions. It has risen to be not only Henan's but also Central China's financial center. The productivity of its financial sector is ranked twelfth among all Chinese cities. Its economic vibrancy is widely acknowledged among government officials and practitioners.

Today's Zhengdong is largely known as a huge success of new city building in Central China, which continues experimenting with forward-looking, city-making strategies. Today, Zhengdong has become Henan's largest flagship development project, demonstrating the province's power to create a massive city with economic vibrancy. Zhengdong continues to be one of Henan's most attractive areas to investors, garnering a total fixed-asset investment of RMB 80.2 billion by 2018. It has received praise from politicians, practitioners, residents, and visitors alike for its modern cityscapes, enjoyable parks, lively public spaces, and vibrant economic activities. Currently, it accommodates about 1.5 million people and over 120,000 enterprises, generating dozens of billions in tax revenues. People from nearby cities and provinces come to Zhengdong to seek opportunities for desirable jobs and high-end lifestyles. Its increasing vibrancy has boosted confidence among governments, developers and residents, all of whom expressed doubts and concerns about the region's growth potential at the beginning. With the maturity of its early clusters, Zhengdong has been targeting the development of a few new clusters and their surrounding high-end neighborhoods. These include a second CBD, a Smart Island, and Baisha, a new cluster. The original plan did not include Baisha. Zhengdong's authority foresaw the new area's potential to further expand eastward and added Baisha to its administrative territory in 2013.

Since 2014 Zhengdong's development priority has shifted from constructing new structures to fostering advanced industries, state-of-art technologies, and cultural tourism. It has formed rapid development mechanisms that are based on clusters of civic centers, educational institutions, SOE headquarters, high-end commercial centers, high-end residential neighborhoods, and advanced service industries (such as finance, technology, and e-commerce). It is worth noting that the original plan by Kurokawa included an industrial cluster with an area of 30 square kilometers. This was equivalent to an "economic and technological development zone" in China. According to China's central land policy, such industrial clusters must be separated from other functional zones. As a result, the proposed industrial cluster was relocated to other areas of Zhengzhou, leaving Zhengdong New District with no designated industrial land.

Zhengdong's Clusters

Kurokawa's winning masterplan consists of six clusters, each with different themes (Figure 6.2): the core CBD area, the core residential area, Dragon Lake area (the second CBD), Longzi Lake university area, science and innovation area, and industrial and technological development area (Xue, Wang, and Tsai 2013).

The pilot cluster is the CBD, which is also the demonstration of the new area and where all new constructions began. The CBD has an area of 345 ha (Figure 6.3, 6.4). Its border is a circle of 1000-meter diameter. High-rise office buildings form two rings surrounding the central area of parks and civic structures, including the Convention and Exhibition Center, the Henan Arts Center, and the Marriott Hotel in the 280-meters tall tower (popularly referred to as the Big Corn). Buildings on the inner row are all 80-meters tall and those on the outer row are 120-meters tall.

The second cluster is the logistics, business, and residential zone with 23 km^2, located on the south side of the CBD. The third cluster centers on the man-made Dragon Lake with its 608-ha of water area, which is indeed even larger than the famous West Lake in Hangzhou. A sub-CBD of 48 hectares protrudes into the lake like a peninsula. Land in this area has the highest value in all of Zhengdong. A 3.7 km-long canal connects the CBD with the sub-CBD, forming the shape of a Chinese

Figure 6.3: Aerial view of the CBD area (this is also the book cover).
Source: Administrative Committee of Zhengdong New District

Figure 6.4: Towers in the CBD area.
Source: Administrative Committee of Zhengdong New District

ruyi (an auspicious icon). The fourth cluster targets higher education, occupying 22 km^2 of land around the Longzi Lake. "Water fingers" penetrate the surrounding area for various institutions. The fifth cluster is a science park of 18 km^2. The sixth cluster is the industrial and technology development zone of 50 km^2. The clusters are constructed according to the ordinal sequence.

In addition to the ideas of an ecological, symbiotic, and metabolic city, which all connect with Western modern ideologies, Eastern and Buddhist cultures greatly influenced Kurokawa. The masterplan's layout, architectural forms, and place-naming adopted traditional Chinese symbols, such as ruyi, dragon, pegoda, traditional courtyards, and canals. The plan for Zhengdong New District received the "best urban planning" award at the World Architects' Congress in Berlin in 2002. All the same the plan for the new city had once been widely criticized by domestic planners and architects. Their criticism concentrated on the emphasis on symbolism and on foreseeable ecological destruction caused by the creation of man-made lakes and canals in Central China, a region with limited natural water bodies.

Measuring Zhengzhou's Urban Vibrancy

Zhengdong New District has grown into an integral part of the City of Zhengzhou, playing a central role in the regions financial systems and greatly contributing to an enhanced urban vibrancy in the city and the region. Zhengdong's growing urban vibrancy can be measured by the increases in its economic productivity, its residents' activities (according to mapping based on cell phone data), the number and variety of its industries, and its public life.

Zhengdong has become the exemplar of Zhengzhou's modernization and Henan's economic growth. In 2017 Henan's urbanization rate had reached 50.2%, up from 20.8% in 1997. Henan's total GDP was RMB 4.5 trillion in 2017, ranked fifth among all provinces in China. In 2018 over 20% of Henan's total GDP came from Zhengzhou, whose GDP had increased by 9.6 times, from RMB 106 billion in 2000 to RMB 1,014 billion in 2018, ranking first among capital cities in China's northern provinces. Zhengzhou's built-up area and population had increased by 3.58 times and 1.96 times, respectively. Zhengzhou's urban activities have grown significantly since 2000 (Figure 6.5 (a), (b)).

Enterprises have been Zhengdong's growth engines, driving its economic vibrancy. Zhengdong experienced a period of rapid growth during which many enterprises started their businesses in the district. In the earliest stage of Zhengdong's development (2001-2003), there were only 32 enterprises in the whole area, one third of which were wholesale enterprises. The total number of enterprises rose to 87 by 2004, 311 by 2007, 1044 by 2010, 2312 by 2014 and 6167 by 2016 (Figure 6.6). The variety of industries has also increased over time. Today, among all the enterprises,

Figure 6.5 (a): Zhengzhou's Urban Vibrancy in 2000.
Source: Administrative Committee of Zhengdong New District
Photo credit: Lei Dong

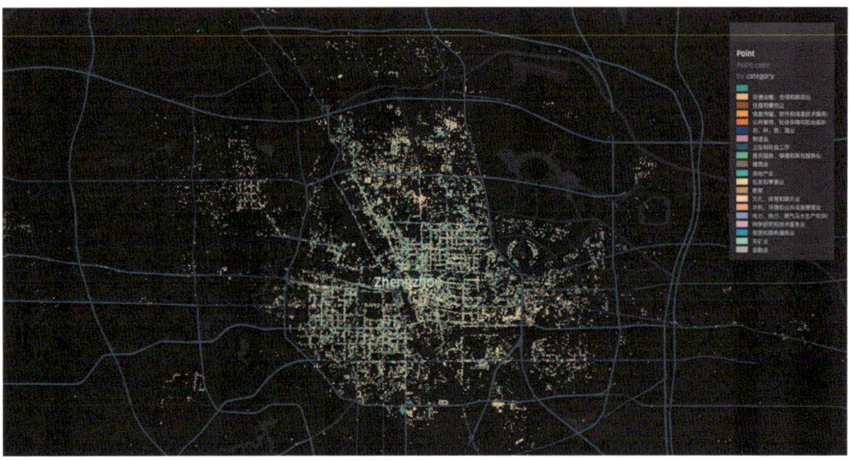

Figure 6.5 (b): Zhengzhou's Urban Vibrancy in 2015.
Source: Administrative Committee of Zhengdong New District
Photo credit: Lei Dong

Zhengdong

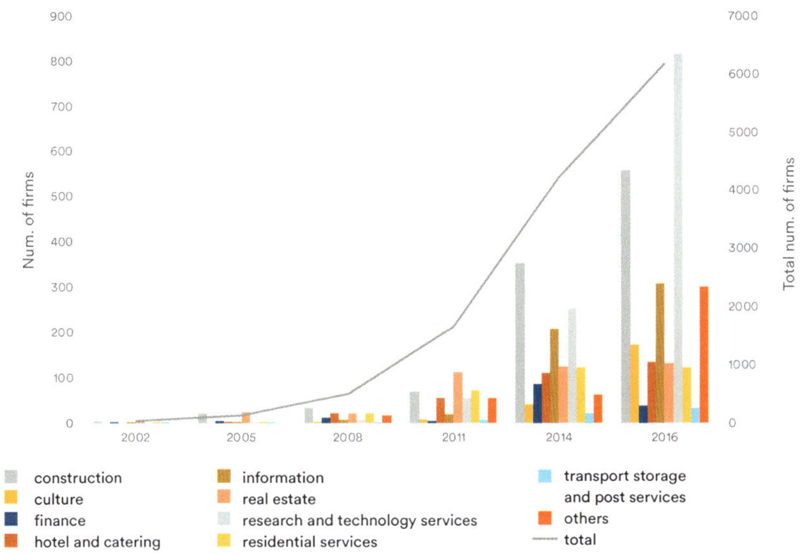

Figure 6.6: Time Trends of Newly Registered Firms in Zhengdong.
Note: Only part of industries are listed

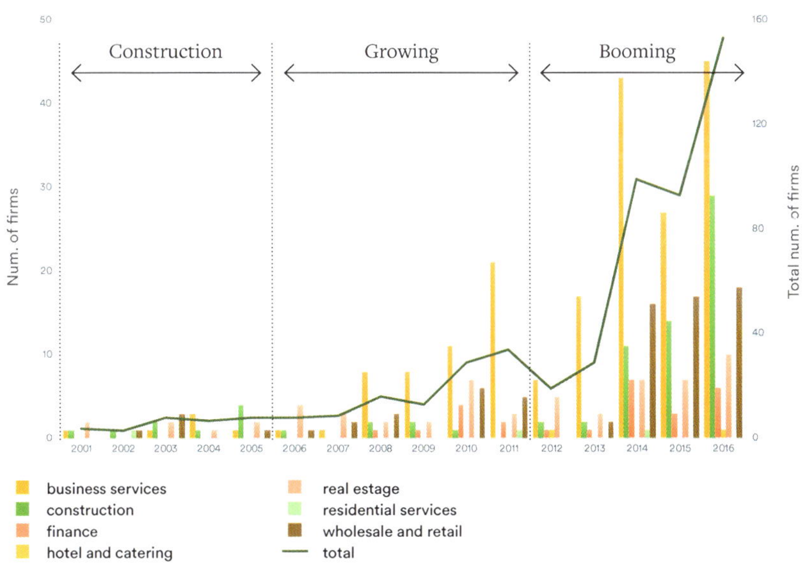

Figure 6.7: Number of Zhengdong's Large-scale Enterprises (Registered capital > 100 million RMB)
Note: Only part of industries are listed

approximately one third belong to the wholesale industry and more than one fifth belong to the business service industry. Other major industries include research and technology, culture, hotel and catering, as well as construction. The registered capital of enterprises ranges from 100,000 to 16.63 billion RMB. The number and variety of large enterprises (whose registered capital exceeds 100 million RMB) also increased over time (Figure 6.7 and Table 6.1). New investments mostly are concentrated in business services, real estate, wholesale and retail. The industrial composition of Zhengdong's enterprises suggests that Zhengdong serves as a cradle to the tertiary industry. Business owners and local officials argue that Zhengdong provides a variety of infrastructure as well as convenient transportation connection to create an environment suitable for business growth and expansion.

Financing the New City Development

In support of Zhengdong's development goals for each phase, by 2008 USD 9 billion had been invested in fixed assets in the region, including USD 160 million from foreign direct investments (FDI) ("Zhengzhou Zhengdong New District Investment Environment Study 2009" n.d.). Between 2008 and 2012 USD 3.89 billion were invested in building Zhengdong's infrastructures ("2008 Nian Zheng Dong Xin Qu Zhu Yao Jing Ji Zhi Biao [2008 Main Economic Indicators of Zhengdong New District]" 2011) (Table 6.2). Zhengdong's major funding sources mainly include land transaction fees, bank loans from China's local government financing vehicles (LGFV), LGFV's Urban Investment Bond, and local government bonds. The majority of Zhengdong's non-operating expenses were allocated to developing its infrastructures. For example, in 2014, ZAC invested USD 43.3 million, around 80% of the government's non-operating expenditure (USD 53.8 million), in infrastructure development.

Zhengdong's development involved several LGFVs founded by Zhengzhou's government. In 2012 Zhengzhou New District Construction Investment Company (ZNDCIC, owned by ZAC) issued an urban investment bond of USD 293.3 million for Zhengdong's development. The interest rate of the bond was 8.1% with a tenure of 7 years. The rating of the bond was "AA", given by Dagong Global Credit Rating Co., Ltd ("He Nan Sheng Zheng Zhou Xin Qu Jian She Tou Zi You Xian Gong Si Gong Si Zhai Quan Ban Nian Du Bao Gao [Zhengzhou New District Construction Investment Company Bond Biannually Report]" 2018). As of September 2018 the remaining balance of all urban investment bonds of Zhengzhou Government was $6.8 billion (Zhou, n.d.). The issuance of local government bonds for land leasing in Zhengzhou started in 2017, and the first year's issuance was around USD 98 million. Local debts are repaid by land leasing fees once the specific parcel is leased. The first year's bond was rated "AAA" by China Bond Rating Co., Ltd. At the provincial level, Henan's municipal government bonds have grown from USD 81 billion to USD 95 billion (Table 6.3).

Table 6.1: Industrial Structure of Zhengdong – Number of Enterprises

	2001		2006		2011		2016	
	All	Large	All	Large	All	Large	All	Large
agriculture			2	1	4	21	19	4
business services	2	1	30	1	267		1,312	45
construction	4	1	9	1	70		559	29
culture			1		7		171	3
education							14	
electricity			2		2		11	2
finance	1		4		6	2	38	6
hotel and catering			2		55		134	1
hydraulic, environment and public service			2				8	7
information	1		4		20		307	7
manufacturing	1		1		6	1	8	1
mine					1		3	2
public health							12	
real estate	7	2	24	4	112	3	131	10
research and technology services	1		6		56	1	817	17
residential services			4		71	1	122	
transport storage and post services					8		33	1
wholesale and retail	14		63	1	914	5	2,165	18
public management							2	
others			3		55		301	

Source: State Administration for Industry and Commerce of China

Table 6.2: Total Investments in Zhengdong's Infrastructure during Its 10-Year Construction.

year	Investments in Infrastructures
before 2008	USD 9 billion
2008	USD 0.27 billion
2009	USD 0.64 billion
2010	USD 0.78 billion
2011	USD 1.16 billion
2012	USD 1.03 billion
total (2002-2012)	USD 12.89 billion

Source: the Government Website of Zhengdong New District; calculation by authors

Table 6.3: Henan's Municipal Government Bonds in 2016, 2017 and 2018

year	Municipal Governments Bonds in Henan Province
2016	USD 81.01 billion
2017	USD 81.36 billion
2018	USD 95.86 billion

Source: China Bond Rating Co., Ltd

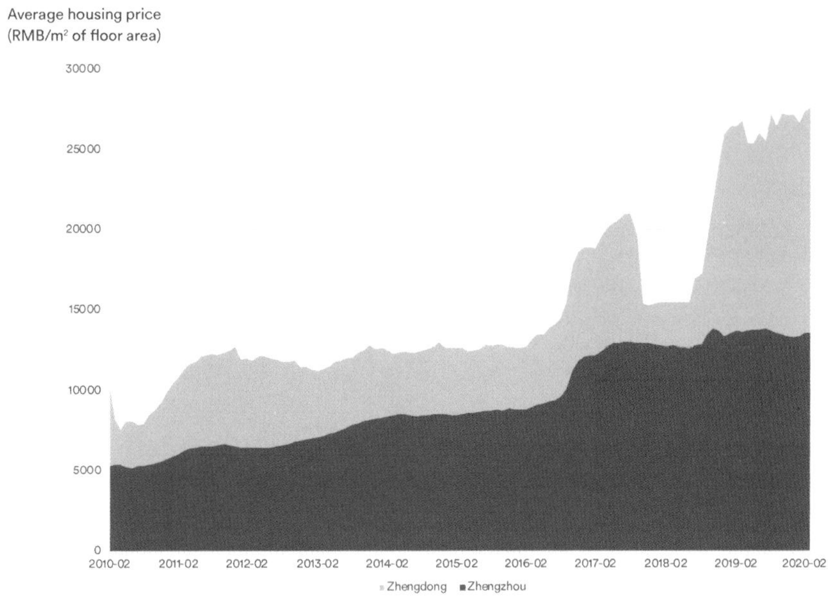

Figure 6.8: Second-hand Housing Price in Zhengdong from 2010 to 2018
Source: Anjuke Henan Information

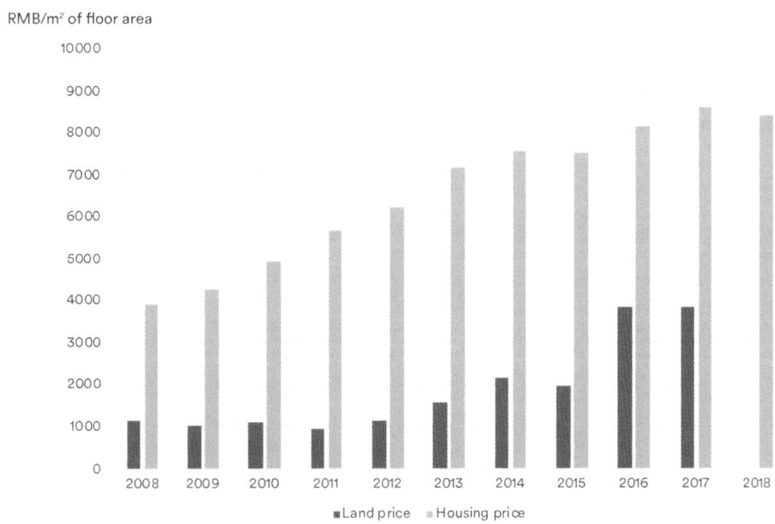

Figure 6.9: Average Selling Price of Commercial Housing Price and Land Price in Zhengzhou
Source: State Information Center (http://www.crei.cn)

Large amounts of investment were made in Zhengdong and stimulated its development. Housing prices and land prices in this area have experienced a rapid and drastic increase (Figure 6.8, 6.9). The average second-hand housing price of Zhengdong in 2010 was about 1,400 USD per square meter. Although it did experience short-run housing price volatility, the price cycle presented strong, positive appreciation trends. Generally speaking, Zhengdong housing prices have tripled in the past 10 years. In 2019 second-hand housing prices in Zhengdong were almost twice as high as the average housing price in Zhengzhou, and the increased rate of Zhengdong's housing prices was greater than that of Zhengzhou. This indicates that Zhengdong is a development engine for the whole city. Land prices and housing prices in Zhengzhou have concomitantly risen with the increase of those in Zhengdong. In the future, with the increase of land prices and housing prices as well as the growth of economic vibrancy in Zhengdong, the unit output of land will continue increasing.

Experiencing A Vibrant City

There is no doubt that today's Zhengdong presents an image of a developed city with vibrant urban activities and modern design quality in its architecture, infrastructure, and landscape. The highlights of Zhengdong impression include, but are not limited to, a visually impressive CBD with a beautiful, central lake, glossy high-rises laid out in circles, spacious urban plazas with views of iconic structures, wide roads and smooth traffic, vast greenbelts running in parallel with major roads and waterways throughout the city, large urban parks with beautiful and well-maintained vegetation, very clean public spaces maintained by diligent workers, and lively recreational life after business hours.

There are currently mainly two ways to enter Zhengdong New District: from the old city and through the high-speed railway station. When leaving the old urban center and approaching Zhengdong on the highways, one is greeted by the iconic image of high-rises in the center of the CBD. The scene is monumental and gives the area a strong identity. Local residents are proud of this new area, calling it the most desirable area in Zhengzhou or even in Henan. Tourists from Zhengzhou and nearby cities flock into Zhengdong to visit the Big Corn and its surrounding parks and civic centers. When entering Zhengdong from the high-speed railway station, one first experiences the convenient transit system, where all modes of ground transportation connect at this station for swift transfers. The areas adjacent to the railway station feature sleek high-rises, including the tallest structure in Zhengzhou, Greenland's headquarters. Driving down the roads in Zhengdong, one can observe wide swaths of greenery between roads and neighborhoods and large areas of parks with delicate landscape design. Trucks that spray water into the air run through the city every hour to reduce dust. All construction sites are surrounded by sprinklers for the same purpose. During the day, the entire area is very clean, ordered, and decorated by greenery and flowers, with maintenance workers taking care of the public infrastructures and urban parks. At night, shopping malls and urban parks are filled with families enjoying leisure activities. In particular, the lakefronts and the ring roads at the center of the CBD, animated by colorful lighting, have become a large outdoors recreational complex. One can observe thousands of people dancing, running, cycling, singing, skating, and strolling, including many club sports with large groups of participants. For school breaks, dozens of school buses from Zhengzhou and nearby cities drive into Zhengdong within a single day, creating records of over 1 million visitors per day during tourism seasons.

Zhengdong's major business areas are full of headquarters of major businesses in high-end service sector. Its industrial parks demonstrate the utilization of the most advanced technologies, such as artificial intelligence for urban management and autonomous vehicles for public transit. Its pilot area—Ruyi Lake Area (the main CBD)—is full of luxurious cars and high-end retailers. Most urban parks in the city are not only lively, recreational spaces for families, tourists, and people doing sports, they are also wildlife sanctuaries. One can hear many birds chirping in their green spaces. Many residents relax in malls, cafes, and parks or meander through the parks, appreciating views of architectural wonders. Every week the amphitheater is used for public education events and charitable performances. Numerous informal gatherings for leisure activities and sports have emerged, scattered across the new area in urban plazas and parks and along major roads. Zhengdong is aiming for a future with advanced industries and happy citizens.

Another factor for Zhengdong's vibrancy is China's development of the high-speed railway network. China saw an expansion of its high-speed railway network over the past few years, with a total length of 29,000 km by the end of 2018, accounting for more than two-thirds of the total high-speed railway in the world (Figure 6.10). This expanded high-speed railway network increases inter-city connectivity and reshapes the geographical distribution of social and economic activities across and within cities. Numerous new city have been planned near railway stations. Not all of the constructed new cities have gained economic activities or promoted the development of their municipalities; some were, or have been, vacant for many years. Zhengdong is one of the most successful new cities that are not only surviving but also experiencing increased productivity and wealth, exerting positive spillover effects to its region. This is partially due to the city's central geographic location.

The City of Zhengzhou sits at the intersection of multiple routes, forming a mi-shaped node (a sort of network of spokes resembling the Chinese character "米"). Zhengzhou has served as a hub of conventional trains for several years, connecting trains traveling across China. On Sept. 28, 2012, Zhengzhou East Railway Station, located in Zhengdong New District, came into operation with the complete opening of the Beijing-Guangzhou High-Speed Railway. Since then, Zhengdong has risen to be a center of China's high-speed railway network, running more than 300 high-speed trains to destinations in different directions every day. It is within a 3-hour radius of over 700 million people. The construction of the new station has greatly accelerated Zhengdong's growth, secured the city's position as a transportation hub, facilitated its connections with other parts of China, and brought about new development opportunities.

Today's Zhengdong is the icon that showcases Henan's prosperity. Henan's provincial government is located in Zhengdong. Zhengdong's economic success, its high-quality built environment, and its government's dedication to urban management have become Henan's demonstration of its capabilities to develop vibrant cities. Higher level officials and officials from other cities and provinces often visit Zhengdong to learn from its experience. Zhengzhou's government is proud that Zhengdong has received acknowledgements from the top. At the Shanghai Cooperation Organization (SCO) Summit in 2015, Premier Li Keqiang led a group of leaders from among SCOs member countries and toured Zhengdong. He introduced the development of the district to foreign leaders at the CBD. Since then, Zhengdong continues to gain prominence as a successful new city development with an international reputation. President Xi Jinping has remarked that Zhengdong is the model for new city development in the future.

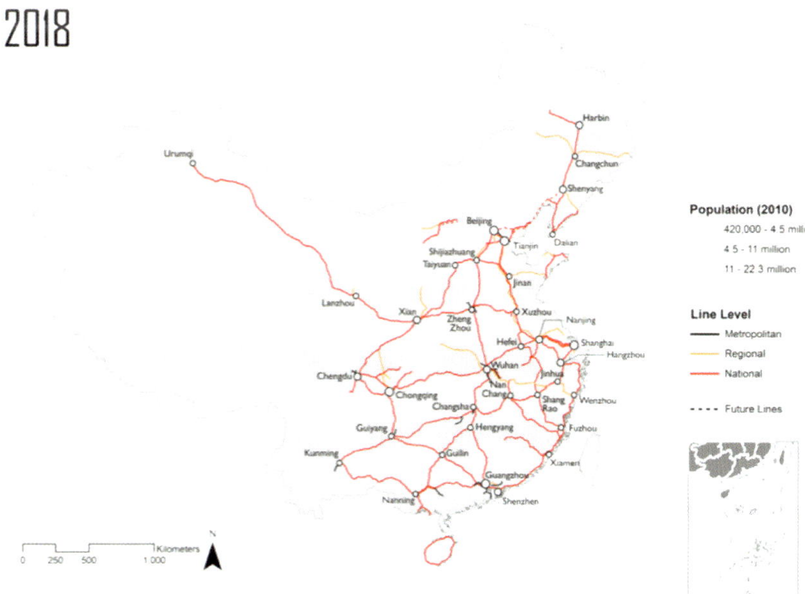

Figure 6.10: China's high-speed railway network in 2018
Source: MIT-China Future City Lab

Two Decades' Effort

How has Zhengdong New District's ambitious blueprint been realized? There are several major strategies that are crucial for the implementation and management of Zhengdong throughout its phased efforts in the past 15 to 20 years.

Local officials believe firmly that the masterplan of Zhengdong New District had set a solid foundation for its growth at the very beginning. The original masterplan was a long-term growth plan with concrete spatial strategies, rather than merely a static, form-based proposal. It is not merely a morphologically deterministic blueprint; rather, it had set the overall structure for a growing city. The idea of multi-clusters allows the city to continue to expand in an organized, phased manner, as opposed to becoming uncoordinated sprawl. Furthermore, it is crucial to the integrity of the new area that generations of local officials have remained consistent and faithful to the original principles during the phases of implementation in the following years. Despite officials' limited terms of office, the implementation of the original principles has been protected by the legislation of the masterplan. This move is unique among China's new city developments. Each new official can concentrate efforts in one cluster without changing the overall principles of the whole new area.

Kurokawa's Metabolist ideal of a modern city utilizes superstructures as the foundation for a growing city. The conceptual relationship among the infrastructures and the urban clusters of his plan aligns well with the collaboration between the public and the private sectors in China's urban development. The public sector invests in infrastructures, including civic centers and urban parks, which enhance the environment and provide urban spaces with better quality; and, in turn, a city with a built environment of better quality can attract residents and institutions, enhance human capital, and boost economic vibrancy. The density of urban population is crucial to the success of businesses. Zhengdong's layout is based on Kurokawa's original calculations of appropriate scales for the clusters and for green spaces. The new area has an appropriate density of population, businesses, and recreational activities and has been fostering key industries within a specific cluster as well as reciprocal relationships among clusters with various target functions. When attracting businesses, the provincial and local governments have created various forms of incentives to invite private investments, to mobilize SOEs to relocate to Zhengdong in corresponding clusters. Nevertheless, all new developments have complied with the overall spatial strategies to realize the envisioned spatial and functional coordination and ensure the area's long-term growth. The coordination of city design and development strategies at intermediate scales between the region and the architecture are crucial to the consistent growth of the new area.

Local officials believe that Zhengdong's development has transitioned from an "urbanization-led industrial growth" to an "industry-facilitated urbanization." The latter marks a new phase of growth, during which the finance sector and the technology services sector will be the dual engines driving economic development. Zhengdong is designated as China's highest-level development zone for smart technologies and free trade, with a special focus on adopting big data analysis and building digital platforms in its management and future development. It is one of the nine "Central Cities" to receive favorable policies for development from the central government. It is also an important member of the "Yellow River Economic Belt" proposed by President Xi Jinping—one economic zone with the same level of political importance as the Yangtze River Basin and the Guangdong-Hong Kong-Macau Greater Bay Area.

The overall development of Zhengdong New District has been led by young officials who are about to be promoted to the provincial level. This reflects the political importance of this area: government workers regard these officials as rising stars, who are well-educated, ambitious, and capable. These young officials are eager to make progress in order to demonstrate their knowledge and capabilities. Government workers and business owners have found it easier to get things done in Zhengdong. On one hand, its officials have created a new environment that is less bureaucratic and more likely to enable progressive changes in the new city. On the other, Zhengdong has designed a policy of "Eight Synchronizations," which has greatly enhanced inter-bureau collaboration and significantly shortened the governmental procedures of project approval. Such synchronizations can help investors and developers significantly cut down costs when entering Zhengdong; hence the new policy has been successful in attracting investments.

Zhengdong's development was also ensured by the massive shanty town clearance at the beginning. Zhengzhou's government cleared the entire area and resettled original residents—mostly rural—early on within the new district in order to avoid speculative protests, ensuring smooth development in the coming years. Local officials are proud that its shanty town clearance has received praises from the central government, specifically China's Ministry of Land and Resources and Ministry of Housing and Urban-Rural Development. The construction of Zhengdong's starting zone began without land transactions. This set a good example for subsequent shanty town clearance, which occurred smoothly in general. This is partially due to the fact that the development of the core area began on the site of the old airport, an area already owned by the state from the start. The rise of Zhengdong's initial clusters has lifted all aboriginal residents out of poverty and given them confidence about their future livelihoods.

Building a new city is a long-term project with plural dimensions of strategies. From generating conceptual design to financing the implementation; from laying infrastructural groundwork to attracting major industrial institutions; from the government's internal collaboration among different administrations to its dedication to delicate, everyday maintenance of the area; Zhengdong has always aimed for the highest quality in order to compete with top-tier cities in China and even with major cities around the world. It is an area that has concentrated local and regional resources, well-established international expertise, and, most importantly, political support from top officials in the region and the country. Such concentrated efforts have generated a privileged area for top-class citizens and enterprises in Central China. Henan's residents are in awe of its political status, its economic success, and its experimentation with new technologies in urban development.

Aiming for an Eco-Smart and Vibrant Future

Zhengdong is currently integrating more advanced spatial design and technologies in the development of its newer clusters. For example, a multi-layered, multi-modal transportation system incorporating digital infrastructure is planned in its second CBD—the Longhu Subcenter; state-of-art technologies and artificial intelligence are to be adopted for public service on its Smart Island; and an eco-tourism zone with landscapes restoring the water systems and showcasing Yellow River Basin cultures is planned in Zhengdong's floodplain area. Zhengdong has been designated as a pilot experiment zone for China's smart-city development. Its goal for the next phase of growth is to integrate digital infrastructure into traditional urban infrastructure and build a virtual platform for data collection and data-aided management in the meantime. In this way, it will collect data that can potentially be analyzed by artificial intelligence for improved public services and urban management.

The convergence of eco- and smart-city strategies is evident in many new city developments today. New city governments emphasize improving eco-environmental quality and using digital technologies to solve urban illnesses. Green-growth approaches, such as pollution mitigation, ecological restoration, environmental monitoring, environmental protection, low-impact development, green finance, and green governance, are currently being explored in concomitance with the upgrade to 5G networks, the construction of digital infrastructure, the installation of sensors and digital surveillance systems, and the collection, storage, and analysis of big data. Zhengdong is still striving to be at the forefront of these realms of urban innovation.

Although Zhengdong is currently experimenting with and exploring future-oriented innovations, it remains a product of twentieth-century planning and growth at its start. Its innovations must be understood in its historical context. Today, China's administrations and institutions that govern its urban development are changing. In 2010, for example, during the planning of Zhengdong's new CBD—Longhu Subcenter, local officials invited Arata Isozaki to redesign the area anchored in low-carbon city principles, incorporating underground highways and autonomous vehicles for Personal Rapid Transit systems. Zhengdong continues exploring innovative approaches to its future development. More research shall be conducted to reveal the complications of building an iconic, top-tier new city such as Zhengdong.

References

"2008 Nian Zheng Dong Xin Qu Zhu Yao Jing Ji Zhi Biao [2008 Main Economic Indicators of Zhengdong New District]." 2011. Zhengdong Administration Committee. December 13, 2011.

Cai Yingyin. 2019. "Yi yu wu tuo bang bian xing ji (ji zheng dong xin qu) [The Transformation of A Utopia on A Foreign Land (The Tale of Zhengdong New District)]." Zhihu. 2019. https://zhuanlan.zhihu.com/p/57790220.

Governa, Francesca, and Angelo Sampieri. 2019. "Urbanisation Processes and New Towns in Contemporary China." *Urban Studies*, September. https://doi.org/10.1177/0042098019860807.

"He Nan Sheng Zheng Zhou Xin Qu Jian She Tou Zi You Xian Gong Si Gong Si Zhai Quan Ban Nian Du Bao Gao [Zhengzhou New District Construction Investment Company Bond Biannually Report]." 2018. China Bond. August 29, 2018. https://www.chinabond.com.cn/cb/cn/ywcz/fxyfxdf/zqzl/qyz/cwbg/20180829/149919876.shtml.

Lin, Zhongjie. 2010. *Kenzo Tange and the Metabolist Movement: Urban Utopias of Modern Japan*. Routledge.

Shepard, Wade. 2015. "'The Gift from the Sea': Through Land Reclamation, China Keeps Growing and Growing." CityMetric. August 25, 2015. https://www.citymetric.com/skylines/gift-sea-through-land-reclamation-china-keeps-growing-and-growing-1350.

Xinhuanet. n.d. "Zhou Ding You: Nu Li Ba Zheng Dong Xin Qu Da Zao Cheng Xin Xing Cheng Zheng Hua Yang Ban [Zhou Dingyou: Striving to Build Zhengdong New District as A Paradigm for New-Type Urbaninzation]." Xinhuanet.Com. Accessed January 9, 2020. http://www.ha.xinhuanet.com/special/special2018/zdyinterview2018/index.htm.

Xue, Charlie QL, Ying Wang, and Luther Tsai. 2013. "Building New Towns in China–A Case Study of Zhengdong New District." *Cities* 30: 223–232.

Ye, Ran. 2019. "Che Di Da Po Gui Cheng Zhi Yi, Zheng Dong Xin Qu Ying Lai Xin Jia Zhi Shi Dai [Refuting the Skepticism of a Ghost City Utterly, Zhengdong New District Welcomes a New Era with New Value]." Fang Tang Think Tank. 2019. http://www.ftzhiku.com/content/1569598210.

"Zhengzhou Zhengdong New District Investment Environment Study 2009." n.d. KPMG. Accessed August 27, 2019. https://www.kpmg.de/media/Zhengzhou_Investment09_eng.pdf.

Zhou, Xiaoqing. n.d. "He Nan Sheng Ji Xia Xia Ge Shi Jing Ji Cai Zheng Shi Li Yu Zhai Wu Yan Jiu (2018) [Economic Conditions and Debts of Henan Province and Its Prefectual Cities]." SHXSJ. http://www.shxsj.com/uploadfile/kanwu/20181214-1.pdf.

Zi, Lili. 2012. "Zheng Dong Xin Qu Di Jia 10 Nian Zeng Zhi Jin 10 Bei [Land Prices in Zhengdong New District Is Tenfold in 10 Years]." News.Ifeng.Com. December 22, 2012. http://news.ifeng.com/gundong/detail_2012_12/22/20419536_0.shtml.

Chapter 7.

Gu'an: Private Planning for Industrial Growth

Angie Jo

In 2002 Gu'an was one of the poorest counties in Hebei Province—with a population of 380,000, annual fiscal revenue of 110 million RMB, and a per capita GDP under USD 1,000—when the Gu'an county government formed a public-private partnership with a real estate developer called China Fortune Land Development (CFLD). CFLD would plan, build, and populate a "new industry city" driven by clusters in three sectors: advanced LED display manufacturing, aviation and aerospace technology, and biomedical R&D, on 60 km^2 of greenfield land. In exchange for creating a new economic engine for the county's long-term growth, CFLD would be given "ownership" of the city for 50 years, during which it could exercise control over all aspects of the city planning process, get first rights access to the land, and split revenue with the local government.

Now, a little over fifteen years into this experimental contract, Gu'an has become the second wealthiest county in Hebei province—its nominal fiscal revenue having jumped an astonishing 90 times from RMB 110 million (USD 16 million) in 2002 to nearly RMB 10 billion (USD 1.5 billion) in 2017[1] ("Gu'an New Industry City" n.d.)—but the private developer *de facto* owns and operates the new city they have built.

What unique planning practices contributed to the industrial activation and economic vibrancy of Gu'an? This chapter highlights the large role of a private developer acting as the central coordinator of a new city project, master-planning not only its physical urban design but also its economic underpinnings. CFLD succeeded in executing three main strategies: taking advantage of the untapped potential in Gu'an's administrative and economic geography (the *where*); setting market-aligned industrial policy backed by research (the *what*); and recruiting firms in priority industries using its large corporate network (the *how*). Using these strategies, CFLD coordinated existing resources to concentrate in one place, allowing them to enjoy the agglomerative benefits of a new industrial cluster. Whether these strategies are unique to Gu'an or how widely these strategies can travel remains an open question that will be tested as CFLD replicates its model throughout and beyond China.

As the story is told in the real estate world, Gu'an sat poised to "catch" the development pressure radiating out from the Beijing-Tianjin industrial belt in the early 2000s. Located 50 km south of Tiananmen Square, it was just an hour's drive from the capital and between two of the largest and most industrious cities in China: Beijing to the north, which would grow from 13 to 30 million people between 2001 and 2016, and Tianjin to the east, which would jump from 5 to 15 million (Xu 2002). As of 2002, however, most developers had passed over Gu'an, dismissing it as a "blank sheet of paper," "a gamble," and "a small county town with the lowest GDP in Hebei province" (Caijing Magazine 2017). In addition, despite its promising location,

1. CFLD urban planning exhibit in Gu'an New Industry City, visited November 2018.

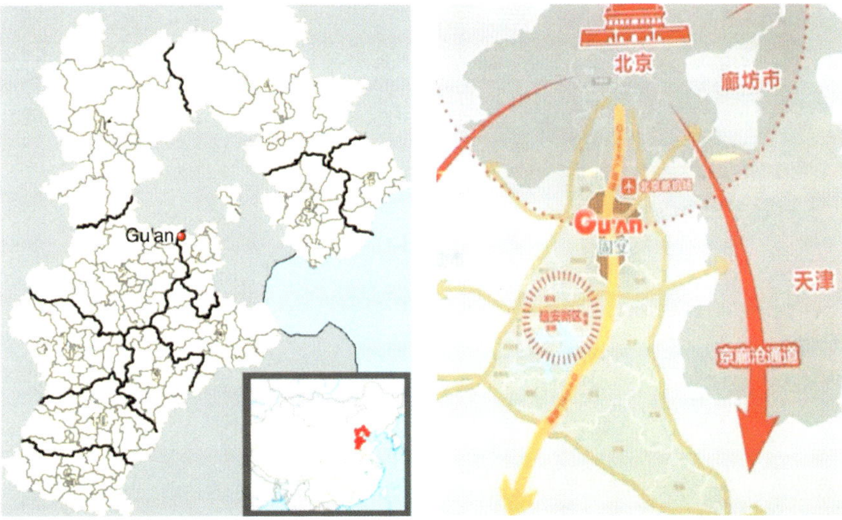

Figure 7.1 & 7.2: The location of Gu'an County in Hebei province on the edge of Beijing and Tianjin.
Sources: Left: Penyulap, Wikipedia Commons
Right: Author's photo from urban planning exhibit, Gu'an New Industry City, Hebei, taken November 2018.

Gu'an was in a separate administrative and fiscal region not sustained by the wealthy mega-cities on its borders. The local government lacked the capital, political clout, corporate connections, and administrative capacity to directly develop urban and industrial projects on its own, and although it controlled vast swathes of cheap and vacant land, the same was true for most greenfield areas within a 50-km radius of Beijing. This did not serve to differentiate Gu'an from the other poor, competing counties around it.

Gu'an's fortunes began to change in 2002 when the county government signed a special PPP contract with CFLD, an early-stage real estate developer. The founder of the company, Wang Wenxue, sought to set it apart from established domestic players that could outcompete CFLD in terms of construction experience and capital horsepower (Caijing Magazine 2017). Instead of offering the Gu'an government the usual menu of residential and commercial products—products that typical developers would construct, sell, and then exit as fast as possible—CFLD proposed an "end-to-end solution" that would help redirect the county's economic trajectory down a more promising path. This meant that CFLD would execute the full suite of traditional urban planning services on behalf of the weak local government, including rural to urban land conversion, land use planning, urban design, infrastructure capitalization and construction, residential and commercial development, public facilities and city services, schools, hospitals, public parks, libraries, transit, business services, and even the branding and "cultural aspects" of the area ("Public-Private

Partnership" n.d.).[2]

But more significantly, CFLD's motto was "Industry First." The company asserted that the only sustainable practice of regional development required not only spatial planning and physical infrastructure investment, but also meticulously programming the economic specialization, sectoral composition, and industrial trajectory of the new city from the start. CFLD argued that it was more important to secure an influx of desirable, high-skilled firms and jobs than to design sleek new buildings. Most importantly, these firms and jobs must come to Gu'an following market logic rather than political pressure or state handouts. If there was no economic rationale for the new city to exist, Gu'an was at risk of becoming yet another bedroom town—or worse, a "ghost town."

A unique PPP

The contract between CFLD and the Gu'an county government was designed to be a win-win partnership. Under this arrangement, CFLD would initially finance and execute all primary physical development at cost. The following year, the government would transfer back to CFLD 115% of its expenses, amounting to a 15% service fee with which CFLD could cover interest on its loans. Second, CFLD would provide strategic, industrial, and spatial master-planning services, which the government would reimburse at 110%. Last, for every company that CFLD brought in to open facilities in Gu'an's industrial zones, the government would pay CFLD a commission fee of 45% of that company's fixed investments in Gu'an. This incentivized CFLD to make industry flourish, as the infrastructure and service reimbursement fees were only enough for CFLD to break even, effectively providing "free" upfront planning and development services to a poor local government. The bulk of its compensation would be tied to its success in attracting private investment and a corporate presence over the long-term. If the city's fiscal revenues did not increase, they would earn no profit.

In turn, the cash-strapped local government would need to sell its only asset, greenfield land, to collect land-use lease fees with which to pay CFLD. Before the arrival of new industrial and residential occupants that the government could tax, cash flow would have to be driven by land-based public financing, which could happen in two ways: the government could sell land to outside developers at a higher price (due to appreciation in value from CFLD's upgrading efforts), or the government could sell the land directly to CFLD at a below-market price (on which CFLD could directly develop housing themselves, and profit off the wider margin).

---

2. Interviews by author with researchers and managers at the CFLD Industrial Research Institute in Beijing, January 2019.

Although both options would benefit CFLD, the second option was particularly attractive. The appeal of a five-decade "ownership" contract is its dynamic flexibility without the financial burden of full ownership. Instead of "land banking"—which most traditional developers practiced to reserve their chance to develop property in the future once values rise, but buy and hold lease rights to the land while it is cheap—CFLD's arrangement with the local government allowed it autonomy over when and where the land would be parceled and to whom it would be allocated (including to itself) over a 50-year period. In terms of timing, this allowed a private planner like CFLD to act more like a government than a developer: it could choose to auction off land to others or tacitly keep it off the market to maintain option value over half a century.

Indeed, other prominent developers in the real estate industry—such as Vanke and Country Garden—try to minimize the amount of time they are involved with any given project, as the high financing cost of holding onto land is risky in the face of market downturns. For example, the CEO of Country Garden infamously demands that architects finish project designs the same day a plot of land is purchased, in order to build and sell housing as fast as humanly possible and rapidly recycle capital (Ko 2018).[3] Financial companies like Credit Suisse have assessed that CFLD's business model is unique, and subject to less volatility from the real estate market (but instead uniquely subject to policy risks from changes to their relationship with partner governments) (Credit Suisse 2014).

From CFLD's perspective, this arrangement was a bold bid to become a market leader in the real estate market by *not* acting like a traditional real estate developer. This gamble in Gu'an succeeded and gave CFLD a distinctive profit-making strategy: in

Table 7.1: Breakdown of CFLD Revenue Stream Profitability (2016)

Revenue Stream	Revenue (USD, millions)	Gross Margin %	Gross Profit (USD, millions)	% of Total Firm Gross Profit
Corporate Solicitation (Commission Fees)	1,646	96%	1,576	60%
Residential Development (Unit Sale)	4,003	21%	824	30%
Other Land Development (Service Fees)	2,369	11%	261	10%
Total	8,018	33%	2,661	100%

Source: CFLD 2016 Annual report, qtd. in "CFLD's Gu'an New Industry City: A New Kind of Public-Private Partnership" (E-House China & Wharton School of Business 2018)

3. Interview by author with CFLD analyst in Shanghai, January 2019.

2016, across all its projects, CFLD's corporate solicitation branch turned a 96% gross margin and constituted 60% of total firm gross profit (earning approximately USD 1.6 billion), while revenue from building residential units only made up 30% of total firm gross profit. In other words, it made more money and more efficient money through being an industry development expert than through selling apartment units. Given this revenue structure, CFLD is not accurately described as a property developer, but more closely resembles "a service provider whose primary client is local government" (E-House China & Wharton School of Business 2018).

This PPP served the Gu'an government's interests as well: it served as an experimental, yet low-risk venture that netted them outside expertise to do the hard work of bringing new industrial activity to its region. As Zhang Shufeng, present executive president of CFLD, put it, "To date, the biggest problem in the development of China's metropolitan area... is that central cities outshine others. The surrounding counties face many difficulties in development. They are short of funds, talent, industry, and essential mechanisms. In addition, they also face a strong siphon effect from central cities" (China Daily 2018). With the partnership of CFLD, the local government did not need to spend money out of pocket or take on more debt in order for this model to work—all the reimbursements and fees paid for themselves through the increase in land value, based on the upfront capital, groundwork upgrades, and services CFLD put in first. This was something that a small municipal government in a weak economic area simply could not do on its own.

Fifteen Years in: Signs of Urban Economic Vibrancy

Within fifteen years Gu'an has transformed from the poorest county in Hebei province to one of the strongest new industrial clusters in the vicinity of Beijing. Even while sharing tax revenue with CFLD (with about 60% going to the county and 40% to the developer in recent years), Gu'an's total fiscal revenue jumped from RMB 90 million [USD 13 million] in 2001 to RMB 9.9 billion [USD 1.5 billion] in 2017—over 90x nominal growth ("Gu'an New Industry City" n.d.). It has gone from a population of 380,000 and a per capita income of slightly under USD 1000 in 2002, to a population of over 500,000 and a per capita income of USD 7000 in 2018—a sevenfold growth (china.org.cn 2018). And while the original site planned for development was 60 km^2, the scope of the project has gradually expanded to more than 170 km^2—170 km^2 of land that cost CFLD RMB 1100 per m^2 in 2002 [USD 160 in today's dollars], to land now holding houses that cost an average of RMB 20,000 per m^2 [USD 3000 today] (Caixin Global 2017).[4]

4. These statistics are all as reported by CFLD in the press and on their website.

CFLD has invested about RMB 32 billion [USD 4.8 billion] into Gu'an, with infrastructure and public services accounting for almost 40% of total investment (CFLD n.d.). CFLD raised initial funding from several sources, including finance leases, trust funds, and bank loans, and in 2017, issued a USD 470 million asset-backed security with an interest rate of around 6.6%, backed by future payments from the Gu'an government. Thus, by bringing CFLD into the project as a private planner acting on behalf of the state, the local government was able to tap private capital markets that it would not otherwise have had access to.

So far, CFLD has constructed 300 kilometers of roads, six water supply plants, four thermal power plants, a sewage disposal plant, two lakes, three parks, 2.3 million m^2 of linked greenways around the city, as well as several public squares, hospitals, high schools, and commercial districts ("Gu'an New Industry City" n.d.). Through its industrial development efforts, 23 industrial clusters have formed, with over 520 companies, 30,000 new jobs, and RMB 150 billion [USD 22 billion] brought into the city ("CFLD: Operator of New Industry Cities" 2019). The three priority sectors—advanced display manufacturing, aerospace and aviation, and biomedical R&D—each have production capacities worth more than RMB 100 billion per year [USD 14.6 billion] (CFLD 2018). In addition, there are research centers and business parks for airport-based logistics, thermal hot springs, modern agriculture, and an incubator for commercializing scientific research from Tsinghua University. There are good restaurants surrounding the lakefront plaza, and children and grandparents strolling in the park.

CFLD would be the first to remind its clients and its critics that "building a new industry city is a long-term endeavor" ("Public-Private Partnership" n.d.). After only 15 out of its 50 contracted years, we cannot yet make conclusive claims about the net economic impact, longer-term trajectory, or counterfactuals of the Gu'an project—CFLD still has another 35 years of work ahead. But so far, Gu'an appears to have created a certain amount of urban and economic vibrancy from greenfield beginnings.

Three Strategies behind Gu'an's Economic Vibrancy and Industrial Growth

1. *Where? Location choice*

Choosing where to locate a new city requires balancing proximity and price: proximity to a dense urban and industrial center makes it easier to capture spillovers when the existing city expands, as firms, workers, and households increasingly seek urban life without the negative externalities associated with large cities. Simultaneously, it must be far enough away to offer lower land prices, which allows planners to use cheap property as incentives to attract firms and to cut the cost of building up from scratch. CFLD prefers peripheral sites located about 50 to 80 kilometers from one of three industrial epi-centers in China: the Beijing-Tianjin belt, the Yangtze River Delta, and the Pearl River Delta[5]—these three regions cover less than 3% of China's landmass, but produce over a third of national GDP and house a fifth of its population (E-House China & Wharton School of Business 2018).

Strategically, CFLD also takes advantage of administrative and political boundaries that cut across these high-potential peripheral regions. Gu'an county enjoyed all of the location benefits of real proximity to Beijing (as the crow flies), but the land was actually owned and controlled by the much poorer, low-capacity Hebei (provincial) and Gu'an (county) governments. CFLD almost always targets these local governments as public partners: they have the legal right to distribute state resources and make significant fiscal and budgetary decisions, but they also lack the capital, capacity, and connections to undertake major development projects alone. CFLD thus offers a high value proposition in these contexts, even at a 45% commission rate.

Of course, part of Gu'an's forward momentum is due to several key developments announced by the central government over the last few years, all of which strengthen Gu'an's geographic position as a new urban and industrial node between Beijing and Tianjin. First was the announcement in 2014 that an integrated urban and economic mega-region would be formed between Beijing, Tianjin, and Hebei province—"Jing-Jin-Ji"—in the image of other competitive global mega-regions such as the Greater Tokyo area or the Boston to DC Northeast corridor. In 2015, Beijing's municipal government formally announced plans to relocate much of its headquarters to the new administrative district of Tongzhou (about an hour's drive from Gu'an). Then, in 2017, the Central Committee of the CCP and the State Council launched the Xiong'an New Area in Hebei (also an hour from Gu'an) as a new planned city that would absorb much of Beijing's non-essential, non-capital functions, and serve as the new economic hub and "innovation demonstration zone" of Jing-Jin-Ji (Taylor 2019; China Briefing 2019).

Thus the conditions that made Gu'an a perfect opportunity for CFLD—the combination of rapid appreciation without accompanying public sector fiscal strength and development capacity in the early 2000s—will be harder to replicate elsewhere. As one real estate expert put it, "nowhere in China is there a place so close to a metropolitan area where land and housing prices were very low and then enjoyed a sharp rise in a short period of time, fueled by urbanization" (Caixin Global 2017).

---

5. Interview by author with a CFLD analyst, in Shanghai, January 2019.

2. *What? Industrial policy*

Once the location for a new city has been set, the next important question becomes what industries should be prioritized in that location. In recent years, "smart specialization"— the idea that not every region can do all things in all industries, and should therefore specialize in domains that build on their existing strengths in order to make the most of returns to "scale, scope, and spillovers" (Foray, David, and Hall 2009; Crespo et al. 2017)—have been adopted in regions like the European Union. However, the million-dollar question is still: Which are the right industries for the right places?

Although CFLD's early industrial research for Gu'an was originally outsourced to consultants like McKinsey and Roland Berger, the company now employs over 5,000 people in its Beijing Industrial Research Institute to do this work in house (2017 Beijing Marathon n.d.). Their research analyzes global, national, and regional industrial trends; factors for innovation and production; and uses "big data" (from remote sensors, satellites, nighttime lights, cellphone usage, public transportation, flights, transactions, consumption, commuting times, demographics) to draw a composite picture of where the "invisible" city center or corridor actually lies in a region of interest.[6] Using these analyses, CFLD composes a "long list" of potential sectors for a new city project. Following additional analyses of South Beijing's factor endowment, international case studies of comparable clusters, and any local comparative advantages that may apply, CFLD narrowed it down to a short list of three pillar industries for Gu'an New Industry City: advanced display manufacturing, aerospace and aviation, and biomedical R&D.[7]

To zoom in on one pillar, CFLD's decision to cultivate advanced display manufacturing (LCD and OLED screens) capitalized on the fact that Chinese makers in this sector had been rapidly gaining global market share since the early 2000s, and aggressively building out new domestic fabrication facilities (or "fabs") to expand their production capacity. However, as an industry, they relied on state support to invest in these capital expenditures—rising Chinese panel makers like BOE, China Star, and Visionox (as well as foreign manufacturers like Samsung and LG that based their manufacturing in China) sought out cheap land and subsidies that would lower the cost of building new fabs (Hsieh 2017). Local governments owned the most important input, land, and were often willing to subsidize these makers in order to reap the political benefits of association with this cutting-edge sector, as well as the higher local GDP and tax income they generated—for example, the Guangzhou, Ordos, and Chongqing governments negotiated with Foxconn, BOE,

---

6. Presentation by industrial researchers at CFLD Industrial Research Institute in Beijing, January 2019.
7. Ibid.

and HKC, respectively, to award them special industrial zones and mining rights in exchange for locating fabs in their region (Hsieh 2017). However, local governments like Gu'an were not well aware of this industry or its needs; CFLD could thus act as an intermediary for this particular sector.

In addition, Gu'an's relative proximity to Beijing allowed makers to connect with R&D resources in the capital. For example, Visionox (the first Chinese manufacturer to develop organic light-emitting diode—OLED—technology, and the first in the world to produce full-screen bendable and foldable active matrix organic light emitting diode—AMOLED—displays) reportedly agreed to locate in Gu'an partly because it had originated from Tsinghua University's OLED Technology Group, and benefited from access to the basic scientific research Tsinghua continued to conduct ("A Milestone for CFLD Industrial Clusters: The Launch of China's First 6th-Generation Fully Flexible AMOLED Production Line" 2018). On this foundation, CFLD was able to build out a supply chain: it selected and successfully solicited BOE Technology Group (a leading panel R&D and manufacturing company) as an anchor in 2006, then drew in more than 30 companies upstream from BOE's manufacturing process, such as Linde Group, Tianmahui LED, and MagicMed (E-House China & Wharton School of Business 2018). After a ten-year period of constructing their first plant complex, BOE decided to expand its production capacity in Gu'an, investing an additional RMB 3 billion [USD 400 million] in 2016 (Caixin Global 2017). Other display makers, such as Eternal Material Technology, Yeolight, and Visionox filled out the cluster, which can now meet the display demands of over 100 million intelligent terminal devices and is valued at over RMB 100 billion [USD 14.5 billion] ("A Milestone for CFLD Industrial Clusters: The Launch of China's First 6th-Generation Fully Flexible AMOLED Production Line" 2018).

CFLD asserts that it is the only real estate institution in China to undertake such a "systematic and scientific" approach to urban and industrial development ("A Milestone for CFLD Industrial Clusters: The Launch of China's First 6th-Generation Fully Flexible AMOLED Production Line" 2018). That said, while private planners like CFLD may produce new cities that are more market-aligned, research-driven, and less prone to state misallocation errors, politics still poses a risk. Managers at CFLD recount that local government officials optimize for political prestige rather than local comparative advantage, and all tend to desire the same "top" sectors—finance, high-tech, fin-tech, bio-tech, big data, advanced manufacturing—with the same handful of "top" firms within those sectors. New cities are thus at risk of over-competing with each over finite resources in sectors that it never made sense for them to have in the first place. Due to their over-concentration and homogeneity, cities planned on the basis of a few select "new economy" sectors may later face the same race-to-the-bottom problems we see in existing cities today.

3. How? Corporate solicitation

Unlike new city projects coordinated by central or sub-national governments—which can use "non-market force" to mandate the movement of government jobs, branches of state-owned enterprises, and public research institutes or universities to seed the economic base of a new city—CFLD could only attract firms to Gu'an using market incentives. The bulk of CFLD's industrial research department—over 3,700 employees out of the total 5,000—is a "corporate solicitation branch" dedicated to this work. The team (which CFLD describes as "global hunters of promising innovative sectors" and "matchmakers" between firms and new cities ("CFLD in Numbers" n.d.)[8]) is primarily responsible for cultivating the developer's corporate networks, keeping tabs on leading firms in target sectors, and inviting them for relocation to CFLD's many new city projects when needed. It also maintains a massive database that lists the operational, supply chain, and input resource needs of close to one million domestic companies, which helps the team make effective solicitations to their corporate contacts (E-House China & Wharton School of Business 2018).

Using these resources, CFLD's aim was first to secure a "big fish"—an anchor firm that "smaller fish" firms would follow into the new city, and firms that could bring large amounts of fixed investment to Gu'an—such as Visionox in the advanced display manufacturing sector; Beidou, a satellite manufacturer; or a state-owned entity like the National Aerospace Center in the aerospace sector.[9] For these highly desirable "flagship" or "first-tier" firms, CFLD conducted one-on-one negotiations wherein they might offer the firm anything from steep discounts on land, to tax breaks, subsidized housing for employees, or office space in one of CFLD's startup incubators.[10] Once these anchor firms were secured, the "smaller fish" firms were offered higher, more standardized prices, or asked to bid for a plot of land if there was enough competitive demand.[11] For example, once BOE Technologies moved into Gu'an, thirty of BOE's upstream suppliers and partners also relocated to Gu'an to stay close to their major client, but BOE reportedly received the best deal on land for being the first mover.[12]

On top of their solicitation and cross-firm coordination services, CFLD also points to its extensive "business services and operations" team that provides customized care to the firms that move in—such as accelerating fulfillment of their administrative tasks (such as tax registration, patent applications, legal and financial

---

8. Interview by author with CFLD analysts in Shanghai and Beijing, January 2019.
9. Interview by author with CFLD analyst in Shanghai, January 2019.
10. Planning process presentation at CFLD Industrial Research Institute in Beijing, January 2019.
11. Interview by author with CFLD analyst in Shanghai, January 2019.
12. Ibid.

consulting), negotiating with the local government for policies that accommodate their preferences, customizing infrastructure and facilities to their specs, sourcing talent and supply inputs, giving SMEs growth advice from industry experts and accelerators, and connecting them to financial institutions, incubators, and capital sources("CFLD in Numbers" n.d.). For example, when an important potential client, Eternal Material Technology (a large OLED manufacturer) raised concerns about cleanroom manufacturing standards, CFLD brought in experts from its existing aerospace clients to help satisfy their specific technical needs, whereas rival industry towns had only offered them land and tax subsidies (E-House China & Wharton School of Business 2018).

In addition, running counter to the idea of targeting big fish in order to attract the small fish, CFLD managers argue that in certain sectors, it is just as important to cultivate a pool of small fish—startups, incubators, accelerators, research institutes—in order to attract the big fish, particularly in industries where large leading players expand through acquisitions of innovative startups, or by investing in distributed sources of basic science or R&D.[13] CFLD calls this the "tech transfer" model of firm recruitment, whereby CFLD leverages its connections with universities and research institutes to identify opportunities to commercialize academic findings, incubates these ventures in a CFLD accelerator, and then invests directly in them as newly-formed startups based in a CFLD new industry city.[14] CFLD hopes to position Gu'an as the tech commercialization center for new innovations coming out of Beijing, as well as a thriving cluster for its established pillar industries.[15]

However, the main unknown is that despite the more than five hundred firms, twenty thousand jobs, and billions of RMB in revenue brought in through CFLD's recruitment efforts, we do not yet know whether there was an expansion of economic activities *on net*, or whether those same firms would have been just as or even more productive in other places. In other words, did the creation of Gu'an lead to genuine, positive-sum growth, or simply a zero-sum reshuffling of resources from locations A, B, and C to location G? Even if all the market actors—firms, workers, investors—freely chose to relocate to Gu'an based on their own individual cost-benefit analyses, projecting a certain amount of gain due to positive spillovers from clustering together, there has not been a study of their actual, realized benefits from agglomeration and the changes in long-term productivity over time. This is an empirical question that researchers can approach in the future, as the new city matures.

13. Planning process presentation at CFLD Industrial Research Institute in Beijing, January 2019.
14. Ibid.
15. Ibid.

A New Model of City-Making?

The Gu'an case reflects a business model for city-making that is being replicated and exported throughout and beyond China: CFLD has since launched over eighty similar "new industry city" projects in thirteen Chinese provinces and at least six other countries (Brunei, Egypt, India, Indonesia, the Philippines, and Vietnam) (Guo 2018). The Gu'an model has also been lauded by China's National State Council, Ministry of Finance, National Development and Reform Commission, and the United Nations Economic Commission for Europe for its apparent success in creating urban economic vibrancy from greenfield conditions ("CFLD: Operator of New Industry Cities" 2019).

These accolades give even more reason to examine the strategies practiced by CFLD and similar "private planners." After all, private planners operate under extremely different parameters than local governments and are bound by different constraints: whereas local governments have a fixed spatial jurisdiction, developers are footloose; local governments often only have enough land and resources to take one shot at building a new city in their respective regions, whereas large developers can learn from multiple iterations; and while politicians also face negative consequences if their new city project fails to produce returns on investment, market-driven private developers go out of business if that occurs. All of these parameters push private developers towards developing more sophisticated methods for ensuring the economic viability and vibrancy of their projects. It is possible that as investment risk is increasingly born by private sector planners, they will increase the quality, not the quantity of new cities built in China. Indeed, CFLD has recently course corrected in light of China's economic slowdown over the past few years, proactively folding projects in western China to consolidate their efforts near the biggest industrial zones around the Beijing-Tianjin, Yangtze River Delta, and Pearl River Delta regions."[16]

That said, this case study shows that CFLD's essential strategy in Gu'an New Industry City was to arbitrage the difference between the strong market fundamentals underlying Gu'an's location, and the inability of the government to leverage their region's potential. In addition, it was able to fill a gap in expertise between a low-capacity, local government and the industrial needs of firms in certain sectors that they were familiar with. Whether this was a singular situation—the right coordinator at the right place and the right time—or a common set of conditions that is prevalent across other contexts is a question that will be answered as more of CFLD's new city projects unfold across Asia.

---

16. Interview by author with CFLD analyst in Shanghai, January 2019.

References

2017 Beijing Marathon. n.d. "About CFLD." Accessed May 21, 2019. http://beijing-marathon.oc.chinarun.com/html/page-8197.html.

"A Milestone for CFLD Industrial Clusters: The Launch of China's First 6th-Generation Fully Flexible AMOLED Production Line." 2018. LED Inside. May 17, 2018. https://www.ledinside.com/news/2018/5/the_launch_of_chinas_first_6th_generation_fully_flexible_amoled_production_line.

Caijing Magazine. 2017. "Hua Xia Xing Fu Shi Ji Kong Zhi Ren Wang Wen Xue Xiao Zhuan [CFLD Boss Wang Wenxue Background]." Caijing Magazine. June 13, 2017. http://finance.sina.com.cn/chanjing/gsnews/2017-06-13/doc-ifyfzfyz3716326.shtml.

Caixin Global. 2017. "Once-Poor County Builds New Model for Property Development." Caixin Global. March 23, 2017. https://www.caixinglobal.com/2017-03-23/once-poor-county-builds-new-model-for-property-development-101069592.html.

CFLD. 2018. "CFLD Calls for Comprehensive Partnerships in Building New Industry Cities." January 31, 2018. http://www.cfldcn.com/en/detail.html?id=19.

CFLD. n.d. "2018 Annual Report." CFLD. Accessed May 21, 2019. http://file.finance.sina.com.cn/211.154.219.97:9494/ MRGG/CNSESH_STOCK/2019/2019-4/2019-04-20/5215578.pdf.

"CFLD in Numbers." n.d. CFLD. Accessed May 21, 2019. http://www.cfldcn.com/en/numbers.html.

"CFLD: Operator of New Industry Cities." 2019. CFLD Presentation to UNESCAP. https://www.unescap.org/sites/default/files/CFLD%20Presentation.pdf.

China Briefing. 2019. "Xiong'an New Area: President Xi's Dream City." March 26, 2019. https://www.china-briefing.com/news/xiongan-new-area-beijing-tianjin-hebei/.

China Daily. 2018. "New Industry Cities Inject New Impetus into County Economies." April 10, 2018. http://www.cfldcn.com/en/detail.html?id=17.

china.org.cn. 2018. "Gu'an New Industry City Touted as PPP Model by UNECE." May 15, 2018. http://www.china.org.cn/cfld/2018-05/15/content_57806873.htm.

Credit Suisse. 2014. "China Fortune Land Development." Asia Pacific/ China Equity Research. https://research-doc.credit-suisse.com/docView?language=ENG&source=ulg&format=PDF&document_id=806437040&serialid=5zOBUBkW axndZiKzj%2BbXKRndkyjbYKUljysGtVK86j0%3D.

Crespo, J., P. A. Balland, R. Boschma, and D. Rigby. 2017. "Regional Diversification Opportunities and Smart Specialization Strategies." *Publications Office of the European Union.*

E-House China & Wharton School of Business. 2018. "CFLD's Gu'an New Industry City: A New Kind of Public-Private Partnership." Knowledge@Wharton. March 2, 2018. https://knowledge.wharton.upenn.edu/article/cflds-guan-new-industry-city-new-kind-public-private-partnership/.

Foray, Dominique, Paul A. David, and Bronwyn Hall. 2009. "Smart Specialisation–the Concept." *Knowledge Economists Policy Brief* 9 (85): 100.

"Gu'an New Industry City." n.d. CFLD. Accessed February 15, 2020. http://www.cfldcn.com/en/nic-guan.html.

Guo, Yiming. 2018. "CFLD Vows Win-Win Cooperation in Overseas Ventures_ china.Org.Cn." China.Org.Cn. May 17, 2018. http://m.china.com.cn/appshare/doc_1_29302_771777.html.

Hsieh, David. 2017. "Market Insight: Display Dynamics - The Rise of Public Private Partnership (PPP) Companies in China." IHS Markit Technology. November 16, 2017. https://technology.ihs.com/597088/display-dynamics-the-rise-of-public-private-partnership-ppp-companies-in-china.

Ko, Tin-Yau. 2018. "Why Country Garden Boss Is Obsessed with Project Development Speed." EJ Insight. April 19, 2018. http://www.ejinsight.com/20180419-why-country-garden-boss-is-obsessed-with-project-development-speed/.

"Public-Private Partnership." n.d. CFLD. Accessed May 21, 2019. http://www.cfldcn.com/en/ppp.html.

Taylor, Jon. 2019. "Five Years on: The Beijing-Tianjin-Hebei Urban Agglomeration." *Asia Dialogue* (blog). March 15, 2019. https://theasiadialogue.com/2019/03/15/five-years-on-the-beijing-tianjin-hebei-urban-agglomeration/.

Xu, Alex. 2002. "Standing Committee Reports on Beijing's Population Growth." October 29, 2002. http://www.china.org.cn/english/2002/Oct/47100.htm.

Chapter 8.

Cyberjaya and Iskandar Puteri: Malaysia's Road-Map for Building New Cities

Victor Jansson[1]

Malaysia has been one of the most active countries in the development of new city projects with relatively good success. Among the first noteworthy projects was establishing of the new administrative capital Putrajaya in 1999, about 25 kilometers from Kuala Lumpur ("Country Profile: Malaysia" n.d.). The country has largely benefited from the experience of its neighbor, the country of Singapore, when planning and executing new city projects with a strong focus on developing industry and attracting FDI. We observe different development models that are an arrangement of public and private investments. In the case of Cyberjaya, discussed in this chapter, the initial investment model even underwent restructuration due to financing difficulties. Financing new city development is one of the most critical aspects of realizing these projects, and a good combination of public and private investment is key to guaranteeing the long-term success of a project. Too strong reliance on private investment might bring some short-term benefits in real estate development, but this could be at the expense of the industry development. Financial planners need to have a good understanding on how to build successful new cities and vibrant economies when designing their financing model, and adopt a flexible attitude in order to be able adjust the model when necessary.

In this chapter we analyze two projects in Malaysia, the cities of Cyberjaya and Iskandar Puteri, which have used very different development strategies. They both nonetheless represent unique examples of projects that have had initial success.

Figure 8.1: The location of Cyberjaya and Iskandar in Malaysia
Source: OpenStreetMap, Louis Charron

1. I am grateful to Yafei Liu for his contribution to the chapter 8 and 9. His expertise in the fields of design and master plan was essential in the research work that was undertaken in each of the cases studied.

Cyberjaya

The development of Cyberjaya was launched in May 1997. It was the brainchild of Dr. Mahathir Mohamad, a former prime minister of Malaysia and came about after the consultancy firm McKinsey suggested that Malaysia build an IT-themed city within the Multimedia Super Corridor (MSC) ("InvestKL" n.d.). MSC is a Special Economic Zone (SEZ) of 750 km^2, which was created to foster the development of the hi-tech industry and was officially launched in 1996 ("MSC Malaysia" 2019). Cyberjaya, 35 km south of downtown Kuala Lumpur, is located at the core of the MSC with a total planned area of 28.9 km^2. The development was phased in two parts of 1430 hectares (14.3 km^2) and 1460 hectares (14.6 km^2) each spread over a period of about 25 years ("Cyberjaya Malaysia" n.d.).

The government agency Multimedia Development Corporation (MDC) was established to oversee the implementation of MSC and Cyberjaya ("Malaysia Digital Economy Corporation" 2019). In contrast, the real estate implementation was privatized in a joint-venture between domestic and foreign companies, in 1996 known as Cyberview Sdn Bhd (Cyberview) ("Cyberjaya Malaysia" n.d.). The shareholders of Cyberview at the time of incorporation include Setia Haruman Sdn Bhd (SHSB, a consortium of developers comprising Renong, Landmarks, MKLand, and Country Heights), NTT (the Japanese telecom service provider), Golden Hope (one of the largest estate and plantation groups in Malaysia), Malaysia Digital Economy Corporation Sdn Bhd (the MSC's management company), Permodalan Nasional Berhad (Malaysian government-linked investment company), and Kumpulan Darul Ehsan Berhad (the investment arm of Selangor State's administration) ("Cyberview Takes Charge as Cyberjaya Mastermind" 2010). During the Asian Financial Crisis in 1997, however, the project ran into financial difficulties and necessitated government intervention ("Cyberjaya Malaysia" n.d.). Cyberview was eventually nationalized by the Ministry of Finance (MoF) acquiring 70% of the venture held by SHSB (55%) and NTT (15%) (as per the current information on the official website, Cyberview has three shareholders: MoF with 92.2%, the real estate arm of Sime Darby, one of the largest company in Malaysia by market capitalization, with 5.17% and the government investment vehicle Permodalan Nasional Berhad with 2.59%). Since then the company has operated as a state-owned entity. Following the restructuration, Cyberview entered into an agreement with SHSB to mandate the real estate consortium as the master developer of Cyberjaya, while Cyberview kept its role as a landowner ("Cyberjaya" 2019). It is important to note that during its history, Cyberview operations followed priorities set by the government in line with the different stages and objectives of the development of Cyberjaya. According to Cyberview's official website, in 1996 Cyberview was given the role of landowner and was tasked with developing the basic infrastructure and enhancing the attractiveness of Cyberjaya. In 2005 Cyberview acted as a facilitator by selling and leasing land, constructing buildings, attract and support ICT (information and communications technology) companies to setup operation in Cyberjaya. In 2011 the company acted as a cybercity manager, with the objective to drive growth of Cyberjaya as an important ICT hub ("Cyberview | Our Story" n.d.). Today, as a self-defined global tech hub ("Cyberview | Our Story" n.d.). enabler, Cyberview is focused on three key services: investor relations services, industry development initiatives, and tech hub development and management services. In the most recent stage of the development, the intention of the government is to create a more sophisticated industrial eco-system and a more vibrant economy ("Cyberview" n.d.).

Unfortunately, many challenges emerged from the initial planning of the city, which, from our analysis, are not in line with the basic principles for the development of vibrant cities. In the master planning we can observe that the project was planned based on a zoning approach, dividing the city into four main zones: the primary zone is the *Enterprise Zone*, which is dedicated for the establishing of MNCs and small to medium-sized, high-tech enterprises; the second, the *Commercial Zone*, was designated for retail and commerce activities, including hotels and shopping malls; the third, the *Residential Zone* is for developing housing; and the last, the *Recreation Zone* includes the cultural center, the lake, and the mosque (Yusof and Van Loon 2012). This top-down elite-oriented zoning, however, is defined by the physical separation of functional spaces such as work, leisure, and living areas. The Enterprise Zone has a prominent central position in this city and makes up about 12% of the total land area of Cyberjaya according to Sepang Local Plan 2025 (in contrast to only 6% of land is planned for the Residential Zone), and reflects the priorities set by the government to develop industries and attract FDI. The supporting residential areas are, however, located at the periphery of the city, resulting in a separation of life and work. Although commercial and public service facilities are located near the Enterprise Zone for the convenience of business people, they are far from the residential areas. Lastly, its recreational places are located at the edge of the city. According to Yusof, N. and van Loon, J., "the rigid zoning of Cyberjaya coupled with the extreme urban sanitation and tight surveillance of gated and guarded communities, imposes negative social experiences on the city inhabitants, users, and visitors in the city, leading to difficulty in stimulating the activity of the retail and entertainment sector" (Yusof and Van Loon 2012), as well as to an increase in car use and emptier pedestrian streets. Nevertheless Cyberjaya still has the chance to overcome the problems and challenges of its the zoning plan: it can adjust the planning of the remaining, available land – according to Cyberjaya's official website, 29% of the land remained vacant ("Cyberjaya Malaysia" n.d.). A mixed-used planning approach should be promoted for the available land to foster the development of a vibrant city.

Cyberjaya is an industry-led new city development ever since the positioning of the project in 1996 through its execution. At its launching the city was positioned as an R&D hub, with the involvement of NTT in MSC in 1997 and the agreement for establishing an R&D center ("NTT's Involvement in Malaysia's Multimedia Super Corridor" n.d.), which was an important anchor investment and a catalyst for the development of industry as well as a marketing tool for investment promotion. The city unexpectedly drew more investment interest from the global shared services and outsourcing (SSO) sector thanks to good infrastructure (e.g. fiber-optic cabling and dual feed power supply) and a multilingual and multicultural workforce, according to Frost & Sullivan's 2007 Global SSO Report. It was probably not such a big surprise knowing that Malaysia was ranked as the third most attractive SSO offshore location after India and China in A.T. Kearney's 2009 Global Services Location Index. By 2010 Cyberjaya had successfully attracted several SSO projects including Shell, OCBC, HSBC and DHL ("MIFC" n.d.), thus creating a vibrant place for business activity and talent attraction.

In 2014 Cyberview released the Cyberjaya Global Technology Hub Blueprint, which evaluated the state of the development of the local technology industries, identified the future opportunities, and drew a roadmap for the development of value-added industries. The blueprint paper recognized challenges for the development of the industry with an immature ecosystem for high-value applied R&D, lack of university-industry commercial partnerships, local companies with limited investment in R&D, and little knowledge transfer between players. The report detailed reasons for those shortcomings, explaining that the limited investment of local companies in R&D is mostly due to the lack of funding, difficulties in attracting and retaining the right talent, and an incomplete ecosystem for research. The lack of successful knowledge transfer is a direct result of the limited interaction between MNCs and local companies and a lack of a culture of sharing between MNCs and government-linked companies (GLCs) with local companies in the city.

As part of the strategic blueprint set by Cyberview, five technology sectors were identified for developing ecosystems and boosting industry vibrancy: ICT technologies (subsegments of information security, creative content technologies, mobile internet, cloud computing, and big data analytics), green technology, biotechnology, wearable technologies and smart grid technology.

During the growth period of the ICT industry from 2003 to 2010 ("Cyberjaya Global Technology Hub Blueprint" n.d.), the city saw a large number of MNCs moving to the area, including Dell, IBM and Ericsson, and, more interestingly, the city experienced the emergence of local start-ups. And with this latter development, the government decided to initiate different programs to promote entrepreneurship and nurture the start-ups ecosystem, such as the Cyberjaya's Living Lab initiative. In 2013 Cyberview established its own business incubation program, named Living Lab, with a first batch of 16 start-ups in the area of mobile applications, games, and social media; shortly after, Malaysian Global Creativity & Innovation Centre (MaGIC) launched a start-up accelerator program in the city as well. There has been a fast and steady growth of start-ups in Cyberjaya, and it is probably one of the reasons the city is often labeled to as the Silicon Valley of Malaysia.

In 2013 Cyberview received a mandate to transform Cyberjaya into a global technology hub. To achieve this, Cyberview identified two key pillars to support these initiatives: the creation of Cyberjaya as a smart city and as a living lab for smart city solutions. This is the blueprint for the next phase of its urban transformation, specifically for the tech ecosystem, which is an important component of a smart city and a vibrant economy. To develop the smart city infrastructure, the city instigated cooperation with leaders in different industry sectors such as MasterCard, Telekom Malaysia Berhad, VADS, Fullrich Malaysia, and Affin Bank Group. This is a good example of public-private sector cooperation for industry promotion and industry upgrade.

In 2017 the city announced it aimed to become the first cashless city with the launch of Malaysia's first community-built e-wallet TaPay, according to the Treasury Ministry Secretary-General, Tan Sri Dr Mohd Irwan Serigar Abdullah. The plan is to reduce dependence on cash transactions to 63% of total transactions and increase the number of e-payment transactions per capita to 200 transactions by 2020 ("Cyberjaya Aims to Be First Cashless City Using E-Wallet TaPay" 2017). Other smart city initiatives include smart traffic lights, water pipe monitoring, streetlight monitoring, illegal parking detection and smart parking solutions. Sustainable development is another important feature of the smart city initiative with technologies such as installing district cooling systems in central areas. Technologies are important enablers of city vibrancy, and comprehensive planning and implementation should be done to maximize their impact.

According to Cyberview, in 2019 Cyberjaya was home to over 800 companies employing about 40,000 knowledge workers and a local population of over 100,000. There is no doubt that the city has had early success in FDI attraction and industry development, and Cyberjaya has the potential to become a regional center for innovation and entrepreneurship and a vibrant city thanks to a strong industry foundation, an important number of education institutions (seven universities with 25,000 on-campus students), fast-growing region (Kuala Lumpur and MSC), and strong government support.

Iskandar Puteri

Iskandar Puteri, formerly known as Nusajaya City, is located in the Johor Bahru District in Johor, Malaysia. The city is strategically located at the southernmost tip of the Malaysian peninsula, 15 km away from Singapore, and is serviced by two international airports and five seaports. The former Prime Minister, Mahathir Mohamad, who initiated the plan to build a bridge between Peninsular Malaysia and Singapore, kicked off the new city project in 1993 ("Iskandar Puteri" 2019). Iskandar Puteri is part of the special economic zone of Iskandar Malaysia, formerly known as Iskandar Development Region, and has a planned area of 367 km^2. Iskandar Malaysia is the main southern development corridor in Johor, which was established in 2006 on an area of 4,749 km^2. The development plan of the area was outlined in the five "Flagship Zones" plan, which comprises an area of 2,216 km^2 (an area three times bigger than Singapore) ("Malaysia's Iskandar Economic Zone to Be Three Times the Size of Singapore: Report" 2017). Four of the Flagship Zones (Flagship Zone A, B, C and D) are located in the Special Economic Corridor (SEC) of Iskandar Puteri-Johor Bahru-Pasir Gudang. Iskandar Puteri was designated as the Flagship Zone B, which was officially launched in 2007, and has a planned development of the Kota Iskandar, Medini Iskandar Malaysia, a medical hub, EduCity, a resort for international tourism, and an industrial logistic cluster and residence ("Iskandar Malaysia" n.d.).

The key advantage of Flagship Zone B is its proximity to Singapore, currently only 40 km from the city state's CBD. And with the construction of the Singapore–Kuala Lumpur High Speed Rail, due for completion in 2026 ("Singapore-KL High Speed Rail Targeted to Start Running by around 2026; Journey Will Take 90 Minutes" 2016), transportation between the two neighboring cities will be further enhanced. It is of course an obvious decision to develop a new city based on its significant geographic advantages. In fact the development of Iskandar Malaysia is undertaken in close cooperation between the two countries, which is a victory for both sides if the project is successfully implemented. Singapore offers a mature business environment, experienced human resources, world-class infrastructure and industrialization experience, whereas Iskandar Malaysia offers land for industrial expansion, abundance of low-cost labor, comparable low-cost living, and government support. As a result we observe a growing trend of companies currently located in Singapore moving their support functions to Iskandar Puteri to benefit from the strong investment environment. In 2016 the government launched the GBS (Global Business Services) Iskandar programme to help companies establishing or expanding their GBS operations in the region (back-office functions such as finance, human resources, IT and call centers) ("All About Iskandar Investments and Projects" n.d.). The programme is managed by i2M Ventures ("Who Is I2M" n.d.), a subsidiary of Khazanah Nasional Berhad (KNB—the strategic investment fund of the government of Malaysia), and has successfully supported the establishment of dozens of projects including KPMG, Frost & Sullivan, Aegis and Courts Asia.

Besides attracting enterprise support centers, Iskandar Puteri has also become a hot spot for businesses serving Singapore, and the surrounding region. In 2016 when VADS Berhad (VADS), a subsidiary of Malaysia Telekom, decided to build the company's largest, purpose-built data center to date in the young city, the reasons were obvious according to Edwin Ng, General Manager of data center services, "VADS is targeting enterprises that may have facilities in Singapore, and are looking to expand into Malaysia. There are also multinational companies, who already have a data center in Singapore, but looking at a conducive base that has a lower cost to set up their infrastructure. Iskandar is the perfect choice to serve them" ("Malaysia's VADS Shares Plans for Nusajaya and Cyberjaya" 2016).

According to a report issued by the Iskandar Regional Development Authority in 2008, Iskandar Puteri's original planning was done in the mid-1990s, but the Asian financial crisis in 1997 stalled the development for several years. In 2003 a revised master plan was approved by the Johor State Government defining a framework that included several catalyst and signature developments, and aiming at creating a city with diversified functional clusters. The key functional clusters include state government housing, industrial parks, logistic parks, medical parks, harbor (offering living, office parks, shopping and recreational spots and waterfront lifestyle activities), education complex, international destination resort, and high-quality residential areas ("Iskandar Malaysia" n.d.).

Iskandar Puteri was planned with social, environmental, and economic sustainability as core features, and it is envisioned to become Malaysia's most connected and livable city according to the city official website, accommodating a population of 500,000 by 2025. In 2012 the city was presented the Best Masterplan Award at the FIABCI Prix d'Excellence Awards ("Nusajaya Wins in Master Plan Category" 2012), which is a testament to the effort invested in the initial planning of the project. It goes without saying that the city master plan is one significant precondition or factor for the project's success and creating a vibrant city.

The new city is at the core development of Iskandar Malaysia with eight signature developments: Kota Iskandar (Johor state's new administrative center), the Southern Industrial and Logistics Clusters (SiLC), Medini, Puteri Harbour Waterfront Development, EduCity, Afiat Healthpark, International Destination Resort, and Nusajaya Residences, which are all aligned with the sectors and industries promoted in the 10th Malaysia Plan (PM10, year 2011 to 2015). The sectors and industries include government, tourism, leisure, education, creative, healthcare and wellness, business and industry, commerce and finance as well as property and infrastructure. Iskandar Puteri has been successful in attracting anchor projects that have had a major boost in its development. Those key investment projects include Legoland Theme Park, Columbia Asia Hospital, Pinewood Studios, Gleneagles Medini Hospital, Sanrio Hello Kitty Town, and international universities clustered in EduCity ("Iskandar Malaysia" n.d.).

EduCity is planned on an area of 300 acres (about 1.2 km^2), it is recognized as an Entry Point Project (EPP) under the National Key Economic Area (NKEA). Newcastle University Medicine Malaysia was the first project established in 2011; it was followed by eight more institutions including the University of Southampton Malaysia, Multimedia University, University of Reading Malaysia, Netherlands Maritime Institute of Technology, Management Development Institute of Singapore, Raffles University Iskandar, Marlborough College Malaysia, and Raffles American School. Those projects in Malaysia were established with the assistance of local partners. Medini Iskandar Malaysia Sdn Bhd (MIM), for example, partnered with the University of Reading and put in charge of investment and operations support ("Medini - Iskandar Malaysia" n.d.). MIM is the master developer of Medini City owned by a joint-venture between KNB and IIB named Jasmine Acres Sdn Bhd (60% shareholder of MIM); Dubai-based, global infrastructure investment and development firm United World Infrastructure (20%); and the Japanese conglomerate Mitsui & Co Ltd (20%) ("Shareholders | Medini" n.d.).

There is no doubt that industry and economic development are a result of promoting investment and implementing it successfully, especially for new city projects. Catalyst projects are important ignitors of economic vibrancy. Some projects can have impacts not only on the economic and industrial activity of the city but also on its cultural, social, and demographic characteristics. The local government clearly understood the importance of promoting investment: to accelerate the development of the area, a special federal statutory body, the Iskandar Regional Development Authority (IRDA), was set up to oversee the overall development of Iskandar Malaysia, including acting as a one-stop approval center for projects settling in the area.

To develop Iskandar Puteri the government mandated three companies as master developers of the 24,000 acres area (97.1 km^2): UEM Sunrise Berhad, Iskandar Investment Berhad (IIB), and Iskandar Waterfront Holdings (IWH) ("Iskandar Puteri" n.d.). UEM Sunrise Berhad is a publicly-listed company and one of Malaysia's top property developers. It is the flagship company for township and property development businesses of UEM Group Berhad, which is a wholly owned entity of Khazanah Nasional Berhad (KNB), the investment-holding arm of the Government of Malaysia. Iskandar Investment Berhad (IIB), formerly known as South Johor Investment Corporation Berhad, incorporated in 2006 to drive the development of Iskandar Malaysia. IIB's shareholding includes KNB (60%), Employees Provident Fund (EPF) (20%) and Kumpulan Prasarana Rakyat Johor Berhad (KPRJ) (20%), a company wholly owned by the Johor State Government. Thanks to a common shareholder in KNB, Malaysian sovereign wealth fund, the two companies have been able to coordinate efforts in the master planning of Iskandar Puteri, and its subsequent construction. According to Agatino Rizzo and John Glasson (Rizzo and Glasson 2012), the initial investment of Iskandar master plan between 2006 and 2010 for Iskandar Malaysia, with Iskandar Puteri as the largest benefactor, was estimated around USD 11.8 billion (RM 47 billion), including infrastructure investment of USD 1 billion (RM 4.3 billion). In order to complete the project in 2025 (the expected completion date of Iskandar Puteri), an additional investment of USD 80.4 billion (RM 335 billion) from the public and private sectors is needed. The major source of the investments include investment from the master developers (e.g. UEM and IIB), GLCs (Government-Linked Companies), and FDI.

Iskandar Waterfront Holdings (IWH) is a Public-Private Partnership (PPP) involving Credence Resources Snd Bhd (private equity) and Kumpulan Prasarana Rakyat Johor Sdn Bhd (KPRJ) (State equity) according to its official website. The Malaysian's Minister of Finance (MoF) is also a strategic partner of IWH through its strategic investment fund Iskandar Waterfront Sdn Bhd, as well as KNB with a minority indirect shareholding. IWH has a total land bank of 4,300 acres (17.4 km^2), most of which is prime waterfront land in Iskandar Malaysia.

UEM Sunrise and IIB are important special purpose vehicles or industry development vehicles through partnerships with the private sector. Both companies can invest in selected strategic and catalytic initiatives through shareholding stakes in joint ventures by either contribution of land or granting a concession or development rights. UEM Sunrise have developed projects in line with the priority sectors of industries identified in the national government's Eleventh Malaysian Plan (11MP, year 2016 to 2020). One method used to fund developments was to enter into joint ventures and collaboration with other developers with more experience in a certain field of activity. More specifically, in 2014 UEM Sunrise entered into a 40:60 joint-venture with Singapore based Ascendas Singbridge Pte Ltd, the leading industrial park developer (acquired by CapitaLand in 2019), to develop Nusajaya Tech Park, an industrial park covering an area of 519 acre (2.1 million m^2) ("Work to Start on Ascendas and UEM Sunrise Project" n.d.). As per the agreement, Ascendas Singbridge oversees the entire real estate process—from design, construction, and project management to ongoing property management and e-infrastructure services.

According to Iskandar Regional Development Authority (IRDA), from 2006 to 2018 Iskandar Malaysia has attracted about USD 68.5 billion (RM 285.3 billion) and created a total of 740,000 jobs in the region, and a population of over 1.9 million. The region is currently apace to reach its objectives as defined in its Comprehensive Development Plan (CDP 2006-2025) and roadmap of reaching a population of 3 million by 2025, including 500,000 in Iskandar Puteri alone.

According to our analysis, the fundamentals behind the success of Iskandar Puteri can be attributed to a series of strategies and implementations, including a rational functional planning of the area, anchor or catalytic project attraction, strong investment promotion activity, master development by state-owned developers, and joint ventures with experienced industry park developers. And in both Cyberjaya and Iskandar Puteri, success can be evaluated by their attractiveness to FDI, population growth and employment, all important indicators for economic vibrancy. In all three categories, both cities have shown distinctive achievements.

References

"All About Iskandar Investments and Projects." n.d. GBS Iskandar. Accessed January 13, 2020. http://gbs-iskandar.my/.

"Country Profile: Malaysia." n.d. Library of Congress. Accessed January 13, 2020. https://webcache.googleusercontent.com/search?q=cache:2H9YUAdXWaQJ:https://www.loc.gov/rr/frd/cs/profiles/Word/Malaysia.doc+&cd=1&hl=en&ct=clnk&gl=ca.

"Cyberjaya." 2019. In *Wikipedia*. https://en.wikipedia.org/w/index.php?title=Cyberjaya&oldid=923233619.

"Cyberjaya Aims to Be First Cashless City Using E-Wallet TaPay." 2017. Borneo Post Online. December 8, 2017. https://www.theborneopost.com/2017/12/08/cyberjaya-aims-to-be-first-cashless-city-using-e-wallet-tapay/.

"Cyberjaya Global Technology Hub Blueprint." n.d. Accessed February 4, 2020. http://www.cyberjayamalaysia.com.my/docs/default-source/default-document-library/global-technology-hub-blueprint.pdf?sfvrsn=2.

"Cyberjaya Malaysia." n.d. Cyberjayamalaysia. Accessed January 13, 2020. http://www.cyberjayamalaysia.com.my/about/the-story.

"Cyberview." n.d. Accessed January 13, 2020. http://cyberview.com.my.

"Cyberview | Our Story." n.d. Accessed February 4, 2020. http://cyberview.com.my/about/our-story.

"Cyberview Takes Charge as Cyberjaya Mastermind." 2010. The Star Online. April 17, 2010. https://www.thestar.com.my/business/business-news/2010/04/17/cyberview-takes-charge-as-cyberjaya-mastermind/.

"InvestKL." n.d. Accessed January 13, 2020. http://www.investkl.gov.my/.

"Iskandar Malaysia." n.d. Iskandar Malaysia. Accessed January 13, 2020. http://iskandarmalaysia.com.my/.

"Iskandar Puteri." 2019. In *Wikipedia*. https://en.wikipedia.org/w/index.php?title=Iskandar_Puteri&oldid=932340184.

"Iskandar Puteri." n.d. Accessed January 13, 2020. http://www.iskandarputeri.com/.

"Malaysia Digital Economy Corporation." 2019. MDEC. June 12, 2019. https://mdec.

my/about-mdec/who-we-are/.

"Malaysia's Iskandar Economic Zone to Be Three Times the Size of Singapore: Report." 2017. Text. The Straits Times. July 3, 2017. https://www.straitstimes.com/asia/se-asia/malaysias-iskandar-economic-zone-to-be-three-times-the-size-of-singapore-report.

"Malaysia's VADS Shares Plans for Nusajaya and Cyberjaya." 2016. August 16, 2016. http://www.vads.com/malaysias-vads-shares-plans-for-nusajaya-and-cyberjaya/.

"Medini - Iskandar Malaysia." n.d. Accessed January 13, 2020. http://www.medini.com.my/.

"MIFC." n.d. Accessed January 13, 2020. http://www.mifc.com/index.php?ch=48&pg=203&ac=115&bb=uploadpdf.

"MSC Malaysia." 2019. In *Wikipedia*. https://en.wikipedia.org/w/index.php?title=MSC_Malaysia&oldid=905695048.

"NTT's Involvement in Malaysia's Multimedia Super Corridor." n.d. Accessed February 4, 2020. https://www.ntt.co.jp/news/news97e/970507.html.

"Nusajaya Wins in Master Plan Category." 2012. The Star Online. May 26, 2012. https://www.thestar.com.my/news/community/2012/05/26/nusajaya-wins-in-master-plan-category.

Rizzo, Agatino, and John Glasson. 2012. "Iskandar Malaysia." *Cities* 29 (6): 417–427.

"Shareholders | Medini." n.d. Accessed January 13, 2020. http://www.medini.com.my/shareholders/.

"Singapore-KL High Speed Rail Targeted to Start Running by around 2026; Journey Will Take 90 Minutes." 2016. Text. The Straits Times. July 19, 2016. https://www.straitstimes.com/singapore/singapore-kl-high-speed-rail-targeted-to-start-running-by-around-2026-journey-will-take-90.

"Who Is I2M." n.d. I2M. Accessed January 13, 2020. http://i2m.com.my/who-is-i2m/.

"Work to Start on Ascendas and UEM Sunrise Project." n.d. Edgeprop.My. Accessed February 4, 2020. https://www.edgeprop.my/content/work-start-ascendas-and-uem-sunrise-project.

Yusof, Norhafezah, and Joost Van Loon. 2012. "Engineering a Global City: The Case of Cyberjaya." *Space and Culture* 15 (4): 298–316.

Chapter 9.

Atal Nagar and Pangyo: Early Evidence of Vibrant New Cities in India and South Korea

Victor Jansson, Angie Jo

Atal Nagar in India

India has a strong case for the development of new cities thanks to a large population of 1.34 billion and an urbanization rate of 34% according to the World Bank (2017). In addition it is important to point out that India has a tradition of planned cities, with New Dehli, a notable example that was built by the British in 1911, and Chandigarh built in 1966, located in the north of the country, and master-planned by the Swiss-French architect and urban planner Le Corbusier. And in the past two decades the private and public sectort have initiated a growing number of new cities projects. Yet, building new cities from scratch does not come without challenges in a country where the land is owned by the private sector and where there are no sovereign funds with deep pockets to invest patiently with little guarantee for return. Prime Minister Narendra Modi has been a strong advocate for the development of cities since he took the office in 2014 (Government of India 2015), and he identified urbanization as an opportunity and a growth engine for the economic development of the country (Puri 2019; ET Bureau 2015). In 2007, while Modi was the chief minister of the state of Gujarat, he launched the Gujarat International Finance Tec-City (GIFT), a new city development located near the state capital of Gandhinagar, which was designed as a regional financial hub to compete with Singapore and Hong Kong (Myers 2018). As Prime Minister of India, Modi launched a smart cities program in 2015 to promote the development of 100 cities in order to improve local living standards and boost economic growth.

During our research of new cities in India we studied the aspects of city planning, financing, sustainability, technology, land pooling, and industry development of many projects. A majority of the new city projects in India are at an early stage of development or remain unfinished as this book goes to press. We have therefore concentrated our attention on the city of Atal Nagar, which has shown interesting breakthroughs in industry development that is in important factor for building vibrant economy.

Atal Nagar, formerly known as Naya Raipur (renamed in 2018), is the capital of the new state of Chhattisgarh that was formed in 2000 from its division of Madhya Pradesh. Establishing the new city 17 km away from the old city of Raipur followed from the state government's wish to develop a modern, hi-tech, eco-friendly city that would serve as the administrative capital of the state and also meet the infrastructural needs of industry and trade in the region. Another major reason for relocating the capital was the burdened, civic infrastructure of old Raipur, which could not support the rapid growth of the State (Naya Raipur Development Authority 2012). Atal Nagar is the first planned capital city of the twenty-first century with a core area of 80 km^2 located in the central part of India and integrated in the Kolkata-Mumbai Industrial Corridor. According to the city development blueprint, the population was expected to reach 560,000 in 2031 (Bahga 2017); however, as per non-official data in 2017, the number of inhabitants in the city was only about 30,000, with a floating

Figure 9.1: The location of Atal Nagar in India
Source: OpenStreetMap, Louis Charron

population of about 100,000 per day (Government of India, n.d.). The majority of the people working in Atal Nagar were still living in the old Raipur, the largest city of Chhattisgarh, preferring to commute instead of relocating closer to their workplace. One of the key reasons was the lack of amenities for daily convenience such as retail outlets, affordable schools, and health care facilities, and the lack of economic activity. But the government recognized those problems and has worked to improve the social infrastructure of the city. In 2018 the central business district was partly built with the government hoping to attract greater business activity to the city.

In order to implement this new city project, the state government created the New Raipur Development Authority (NRDA) to oversee all development works. Owing to the prestigious status of this project (involvement of the country leaders), the NRDA spent more than five years planning the city with the help of prominent architects.

According to the development plan, Atal Nagar was envisioned as a modern city that would focus on socio-economic and cultural life for the state of Chhattisgarh, and integrate concepts of ecology, health, efficiency, and modernity. According to the master plan produced in 2006 (Chatterjee and Mazumder 2008), the functional zoning of the area was planned as follow: green land or recreational (26.7%), public and semipublic (23.0%), residential (26.4%), commercial-retail (1.8%), commercial-wholesale (1.6%), industrial (2.4%), special industry (3.3%), transportation (12.6%), and composite use-zone including residential, commercial, and industrial uses (2.2%). To shape the city into an eco-oriented development, the master plan of Atal Nagar assigned about 27% of the total land to green land—Atal Nagar has the unique feature among Indian cities of having a 500-meter wide green belt around it. Inside the city, the green areas include parks, urban forests, theme parks, sports complexes, golf courses, etc. In addition, an important effort has been put into linking its bodies of water, which combined with the large green areas makes it a truly "green city" ("Naya Raipur Development Plan – 2031," n.d.).

Atal Nagar is planned to be the first greenfield, transit-oriented development (TOD) city in India (Traffic Infra Tech Magazine 2013), which emphasizes the integration of land use and transportation planning and the development of a mixed, high-density, high-efficiency area within a 600m-radius of public transport. The TOD idea is enabled by the linear form of master plan, in which the proposed rail-based, medium-capacity transport system would support the development of several functional areas on the north-south green activity corridor. According to the Naya Raipur Development Plan 2031, at the center of the green activity corridor, are located the Capitol Complex (a huge compound consisting of the Mantralaya) and the Central Secretariat (serving as an administrative edifice of Chhattisgarh state), which are located next to the CBD. Industrial parks were also integrated in the city planning ("Naya Raipur Development Plan – 2031," n.d.).

The NRDA is responsible for land procurement in Atal Nagar in accordance with the Naya Raipur Development Plan 2031. The land up for development has a total area of 222 km^2, or 317 km^2 if including the wide green belt divided in different segments as part of the phasing of the project and functional positioning of the different areas. Until 2018 the NRDA procured over 100 km^2, of which 49% through mutual consents with farmers and landlords, 40% transferred from the Chhattisgarh Government, and 11% through land acquisition. Land acquisition or land assembly is certainly one of the most controversial aspect of new city developments; but there are examples of successful methods such as the case of Amaravati Capital City Development Project, located in the State of Andhra Pradesh on the banks of the Krishna River and built in three phases stretching over an area of 217 km^2. In this case the government implemented a voluntary land-pooling scheme (LPS) for the land assembly that involved over 25,000 farmers and over 33,000 acres (134 km^2)[1]. The landowners were not displaced but became part of the economic growth and benefited from the city development both socially and economically. The farmers were promised by the Government of Andhra Pradesh future developed land plots (smaller than their existing land), a pension, and an annuity as well as other social benefits such as access to health care and education. The LPS started in January 2015 and took 3 years to complete. The government went through LPS notification and consents, verification of title, masterplan and plot allotment policy, plan layout and lottery (Maganti 2019). While the farmers in Amaravati would get their developed plot in ten years, the land price would have increased significantly.

Atal Nagar, thanks to its central location in the country as well as its integration in the Kolkata-Mumbai Industrial Corridor is widely seen as an important trade and logistics hub of the future. Seeking to build a vibrant city, industry development is

1. Pooling Land for Development in Andhra Pradesh, July 13, 2018, https://crda.ap.gov.in/apcrdacommuni/Media/APCRDADOCS/LPS/2018/JUL/

one of the key priorities of the local and state governments for the development of the new state capital. The city's plan includes a hub for special industry development specifically designed for the IT and IT-enabled services (ITeS) and other services in the banking, automobile, and logistics industries and a Special Economic Zone for gems and jewelry trading and processing (Naya Raipur Development Authority, n.d.).

In 2014 the state government and the Ministry of Electronics and Information Technology approved establishing of Electronic Manufacturing Cluster (EMC) on 70 acres of land (about 280,000 m^2) for the initial phase in Atal Nagar ("EMC Official Website" n.d.). The government mandated the state-owned Chhattisgarh State Industrial Development Corporation (CSIDC) to establish the EMC within a period of three years. CSIDC, a nodal agency of the State, facilitates and promotes industrial development, allocates land to industries, initiates programs for entrepreneurship development and people training and sets up public private partnerships (PPPs) according to the official website ("CSIDC Official Website" n.d.). EMC was inaugurated in 2016 and has become one of the major projects of industrial development in the city; it is located in a prime location only 10 min drive from the airport, within 1 km of the city railway station and 10 km away from a logistics hub. In order to attract investments, the government issued special policies in 2014 for a period of 5 years under the IT/ITeS and electronics policies including fixed capital investment subsidies, interest subsidies, rebates on land premium, exemptions on CST and entry taxes, subsidies regarding bandwidth utilization, concessions on built-up spaces, and electricity duty exemptions, to name a few.[2] EMC succeeded as soon as it signed the investment agreements between the government of Chhattisgarh and three electronics companies in 2017 (Smartron India, Forstar Techno Solutions, and Wattson Electronics) ("C'garh Govt Signs Four MoU with Private Players" 2017). Smartron India would set up a manufacturing unit of smart phones and other smart devices; Forstar Techno Solutions would establish assembly plants for tablets, desktop PCs, smart phones, biometric devices, netbooks, and notebooks; and Wattson Electronics would manufacture consumer and industrial electronics products. Mahesh Lingareddy, the founder and chairman of Smartron said, "Smartron is building India's first global technology OEM brand with a focus on innovation led product ecosystem around tronX, an AI powered IOT platform delivering intelligent experiences through a range of smart devices to various verticals ("Smartron, Chhattisgarh Govt. Sign MoU to Incorporate Smart Technologies in State" 2017). Smartron's ambition to become the first Indian consumer tech company to go global by building a robust IoT ecosystem." (Mallick 2017)

The current ICT policies, State Electronics, IT & ITeS Policy 2014-19 and

2. EMC special policies for the period 2014 to 2019 ("Electronic Manufacturing Cluster, Naya Raipur," n.d.)

Chhattisgarh's Innovation and Entrepreneurship Development Policy, have been instrumental in facilitating the development of the ICT ecosystem: they offered an attractive investment environment. It is not surprising that the state was ranked 4th by the DIPP (Department of Industrial Policy and Promotion) in 2016 for ease of doing business in India (Department of Industrial Policy and Promotion, n.d.). Several technology companies have selected Atal Nagar in recent years as the site of their production centers, namely top business process outsourcing (BPO) companies such as HGS, PatraBPO, NextWealth. A state-of-the-art, tier-4, data center was also recently located in the city ("EMC: IT & ITeS" n.d.).

In 2015 Prime Minister Narendra Modi launched the "100 Smart Cities Mission," an urban renewal and retrofitting program of the Government of India with the mission to develop 100 citizen- friendly and sustainable cities across the country. The program would last five years: each state or union territory would nominate at least one city to participate in the challenge. Between 2017 and 2022 the central and state governments would provide financial aid to the participating cities. The plan is for the mission to reveal its results starting in 2022 ("Smart Cities of India- Mission 2022" 2018).

Three cities in the State of Chhattisgarh came under the "Smart Cities Mission" program: Raipur, Atal Nagar, and Bilaspur. Atal Nagar was in fact one of the first cities to launch an integrated greenfield smart city, inaugurated by Indian's Prime Minister in 2018 ("Smart Cities Council India | News" n.d.). Schneider Electric was awarded a contract in 2017, together with the consortium partner IL&FS Technologies. According to Schneider Electric's website this city-project includes the implementation of the integrated Command and Control Centre (CCC) and its overall integration, covering transportation, surveillance, citizen applications, along with utility management system (Electrical and Water SCADA) and intelligent Building Management System (BMS). Other technology enables services available to the citizens: smart lighting, smart transportation, and smart traffic management ("Schneider Electric to Make India's First Integrated Green Field Smart City Project in Naya Raipur a Reality" n.d.).

Before starting its Smart City project, the Atal Nagar's government officials surveyed several cities globally (e. g. London, Amsterdam, and Seoul) to study their best practices and get some inspiration from them. In the end, the city decided to take Barcelona as its model because the Smart City vision to "improve citizen's well-being and quality of life" and of "economic progress" aligned most closely with Atal Nagar's vision and blueprint (Government of India, n.d.). The ICT master plan for the city of Barcelona covers several aspects including city architecture, city networks, city command & control centers, government administration and smart city vertical and horizontal projects.

Pangyo Techno-Valley in Gyeounggi-do, South Korea

A major component of South Korea's modern development in the twentieth century was the building of new cities, which absorbed industrial and residential growth as the country's urban population jumped from less than 30% in 1960 to 80% in 2000.[3] Owing to the enormous magnetic pull of the Seoul Capital Area in the northwest—which covers only 12% of the country's land area but houses nearly half the national population (over 25 million) and generates half the national GDP—the South Korean government has experimented with new cities for decades as a way to redistribute industrial assets and the potential for economic growth more evenly in regions far from the capital. In the twenty-first century, we continue to see a mix of new city models being attempted, such as Songdo City—a private development built on land reclaimed from the sea, which aims to become a logistics and business services hub near Incheon International Airport—and Sejong City, a public development founded in 2007 as the new administrative capital of South Korea for the purposes of easing population and real estate pressure off Seoul and encouraging development in the central provinces of the country. While Songdo and Sejong are the most internationally well-known examples of new city projects in South Korea, however, neither has achieved high levels of economic vibrancy. Songdo is slowly attracting residents and businesses, and Sejong is a government city that was not explicitly planned to house secondary industries from the start. Both speak to the difficulties of inducing economic vibrancy, for both private and publicly planned new city projects.

A clear exception to this pattern is the new city of Pangyo in Gyeounggi Province and the industrial cluster at its center, known as Pangyo Techno-Valley. Although little known outside South Korea, Pangyo Techno-Valley has become known as the new Silicon Valley for emerging IT, gaming, bio-medical, and R&D firms in the country. Developed between 2003 and 2015 by the government of Gyeounggi Province—costing approximately KRW 5.3 trillion for land acquisition and KRW 3.9 trillion for construction (Pangyo Techno Valley website n.d.)—Pangyo was converted from a protected green belt zone, originally covered in rice paddies and forest, to a new city of 3.3 km^2. It is now home to some of Korea's brightest young companies and corporate consortia, including Naver, Kakao, NCSoft, and Korea BioPark ("Pangyo Techno Valley website" n.d.). Featuring low-density housing, abundant green space, and a concentrated IT, bio-tech, and R&D district of just 662,000 m^2, the more than one thousand companies hosted by the cluster generated KRW 80 trillion (USD 68 billion) in revenue in 2017 ("Statistics of Tenant Companies" n.d.).

---

3. Republic of Korea, urban population (% of total population) (Population Division - United Nations 2018).
4. Author interview with senior manager in the Pangyo Cluster Team, Gyeounggi-do Business and Science Accelerator, Jan. 7, 2019.

Figure 9.2: The location of Pangyo in South Korea
Source: OpenStreetMap, Louis Charron

Of several new cities planned in South Korea over the past twenty years, Pangyo is one of the few successful cases of cluster formation directed by a local government. Because South Korea's economic geography revolves around the enormous gravitational pull of Seoul, Pangyo's location just 13 kilometers south of the Gangnam district, the financial heart of the city, and in proximity to Seoul's residential satellite towns made it a desirable site for relocating firms. Thanks to strong market demand, the provincial government had the luxury of administering a strict selection process for incoming firms and prioritizing emerging industries that would benefit from space in a new agglomeration outside of Seoul.[4] Now that the first Techno-Valley (PTV 1) is fully occupied and operational, the province is building two additional Techno-Valleys adjacent to the first, and other localities have launched similar projects of their own. It is likely that PTV 1 owes its success to its singular location—formerly protected greenfield land just south of Seoul newly released for development—in addition to its innovative cluster development model, which may pose difficulties for other regional governments attempting to replicate its success elsewhere.

In 2000 Pangyo started as a national "new town" residential project intended to relieve the Seoul metropolitan area's real estate and housing pressure, much as the "bedroom towns" of Bundang and Ilsan had done in the early 1990s.[5] Jumping at this opportunity for development, Gyeounggi province's governor, Chamber of Commerce, and civil society groups publicly campaigned to reserve part of the land for new industries rather than solely for housing. Their argument was that Seoul was too expensive and saturated for emerging firms to take hold, that Pangyo's peripheral location would allow firms to access talent and collaborations with businesses and resources in Gangnam, and that preexisting industrial and transit infrastructure (good connections to two major highways, the Yongin-Seoul expressway, and the

---

5. Author interview with senior manager in the Gyeounggi Provincial Government Department of Planning, Jan. 9, 2019.

potential to extend a high-speed subway line) made building a new "Silicon Valley" in Gyeounggi a logical national investment—not only for the province's growth, but also to drive the entire country's economic frontier forward.[6]

Historically, the central government of South Korea has led several attempts to use planned cities to redistribute population and rebalance economic activity throughout the country in order to weaken the monocentric power of Seoul. In 2007, for example, the national "Innocity" policy moved 90% of public institutions and over forty thousand employees out of the capital to shore up declining older cities in every province (Lee, Noh, and Seul 2017). But while this massive relocation effort boosted local tax bases and local employee recruitment, scattering these seeds failed to stimulate new clusters of innovative firms around them. In addition, with Korea's national economy and political sphere dominated by a handful of powerful conglomerates known as chaebol, the central government has constantly struggled to diversify the economy through cultivating small and medium enterprises (SMEs) and R&D outside the existing conglomerate complex (Lee, Noh, and Seul 2017).

For these reasons, the Pangyo Techno-Valley project gained both the support of President Geun-hye Park's administration at the national level, and the leadership of the provincial government at the local level. Gyeounggi province bought the land from the state-owned Korea Land and Housing Corporation, and the Gyeounggi Urban Innovation Corporation financed the initial upgrading.[7] Lots in Techno Valley were then sold at fixed prices to large private companies, consortia of smaller companies, or developers to build individually (Gyeounggi Provincial Government n.d.). As the greenfield land initially had high market value as soon as it was released for development, the Gyeounggi government was able to profit from land sales even while offering prices below market rate.[8] The profits from land sales were earmarked for recycling solely back into the Pangyo city project rather than funneled into more general public funds; this policy provided the means for the local government to build a Creative Economy Center, Global R&D Center, and a start-up campus; to fund supportive services for firms within PTV, such as cultural activities and daycare for employees; to subsidize down payments for promising young companies; and to seed the PTV2 and PTV3 expansions following the success of PTV1.[9]

6. Ibid.

7. Author interview with senior manager in the Gyeounggi Provincial Government Department of Planning, Jan. 9, 2019.

8. Author interview with representative from Pangyo Techno-Valley Sales and Lease Division, Jan. 8, 2019.

9. Ibid

Building a New Industry Cluster

A key feature of publicly developed new cities in Korea is that the urban and industrial planning process is heavily guided by an expert review committee, rather than dictated by local politicians or bureaucrats alone. In Pangyo's case, it was a committee of fifteen local government officials, urban planners, academics, and experts in entrepreneurship and industry.[10] For Techno-Valley, this committee prioritized several sub-sectors focused on R&D in "next generation growth engine industries in IT, BT (bio-tech), NT (nano-tech), and CT (culture-tech)" (Gyeounggi Provincial Government n.d.), which included mobile communications, smart homes and systems, internet servers, digital content, HD digital media and broadcasting, robotics, advanced displays, semiconductors, nano-synthesis devices, batteries, future cars, broadband convergence services, telematics, ubiquitous sensors, broadband and networks, advanced computing, wearables, RFID/USN devices, and foundational medical sciences.[11]

The committee first divided the land by function and by sector, clustering genomics—and helping smaller firms in similar fields coordinate with each other via consortia that could collectively buy a larger lot—such as Korea Bio Park, which is made up of 22 companies and takes up three adjacent buildings.[12] Land was then sold in three tiers: 1) Invitational land, which was offered significantly below market rate (about USD 1800 per m^2) to desirable anchor companies and publicly-funded R&D institutes, which were also supported with subsidies for expensive lab equipment; 2) General land, which was sold to individual firms and consortia at USD 2200 per m^2 for industrial use; and 3) Commercial land, sold to developers building office units for rent at USD 3800 per m^2.[13] Unlike other new city projects where land is parcelled and auctioned to the highest bidder, or sold in one-on-one negotiations with each interested company at the discretion of the central planner, prices in Pangyo were more or less fixed within each bracket, and few extra incentives were used to attract firms; the project primarily relied on the inherent attractiveness of the location rather than government handouts.[14] Firms reported that their primary interest was in real estate in the beginning, before they knew what other firms would move into the cluster: they were essentially choosing between renting a floor in Gangnam, downtown Seoul, and owning an entire building of their own in neighbouring Pangyo.[15]

---

10. Author interview with senior manager of Born2Global Startup Accelerator, Korean Ministry of Science and ICT, Dec. 18, 2018.
11. Ibid.
12. Author interview with senior manager in the Gyeounggi Provincial Government Department of Planning, Jan. 9, 2019.
13. Ibid
14. Author interview with senior manager at Dasan and Handisoft (corporate tenants in Pangyo Techno-Valley 1), Jan. 11, 2018.
15. Ibid

In fact, demand was so strong that there was, on average, a six-to-one competition for each lot, which required the committee to stringently evaluate and rank each applicant on a point-based rubric according to the following features: the nature of each applicant's business, its corporate vision and ten-year plan, its scale of R&D, its patents and IP rights, its technicians, facilities and equipment, as well as its financial soundness, business feasibility, and independent risk analysis.[16] The Gyeounggi government emphasized that it was not interested in using the land to extract the most land lucrative sales, but in the long-term health of the industrial cluster. Without an appropriate bid, vacant lots would remain vacant until the next round. The government also prevented businesses from using their Pangyo property as a bid for real estate by prohibiting them from selling the lot for ten years (until 2020) and from changing the economic activities they had committed to in their application for twenty years (until 2030).[17] This firm hand on policy—and the impartial guidance of the expert planning committee—prevented the project from being captured by speculators in the short run, and kept it on track towards becoming a functioning, industrial cluster in the long run.

Economic and Urban Vibrancy Outcomes

When Techno-Valley first opened for business in 2011, it started with only 82 companies, and first-year sales reached just KRW 5 trillion (USD 4.3 billion) (Gyeounggi Provincial Government n.d.). But by 2015 the space had grown to support 1121 companies, over 70,500 employees, and generated over KRW 70 trillion in total sales, accounting for 23% of the province's regional GDP (Gyeounggi Provincial Government n.d.). So far it looks as though the cluster is achieving the regional government's goals of creating an innovation hub that cultivates the start-ups, SMEs, and young talent of the next generation: IT startups account for over 90% of firms in Pangyo, and workers in their twenties and thirties make up 72% of the total workforce (Hee Seok Choi 2016)—a bright spot given the highest youth unemployment rates seen in South Korea in recent years.

By sector, IT comprises about 77% of total companies, followed by BT (bio-technology) at 12%; CT (cultural technology) and NT (nano-technology) make up the rest ("Statistics of Tenant Companies" n.d.). Pangyo benefited from support from the central government, which helped move large public and semi-public research institutes to the new city before the arrival of private firms. Among them are the Korea Advanced Institute of Science and Technology (KAIST), the national

16. Author interview with senior manager in the Gyeounggi Provincial Government Department of Planning, Jan. 9, 2019

17. Author interview with senior manager in the Pangyo Cluster Team, Gyeounggi-do Business and Science Accelerator, Jan. 7, 2019.

Electronics and Telecommunications Research Institute (ETRI), the Software Policy and Research Institute (SPRI), the Global R&D Center, and branches of the Korean Electronic Technology Institute (KETI). In addition, government agencies like the Gyeounggi Institute of Science and Technology Promotion and the Center for Creative Economy and Innovation streamline services for start-ups and businesses in PTV (Lee, Noh, and Seul 2017).

Some of the largest IT firms in Korea have set up headquarters or branches in PTV, including Ahn Lab (online security software), NHN (Naver, or the Google of Korea), Kakao (the country's largest social network and messaging service), SIGONG Tech, LIG, and branches of foreign giants like Apple and Google ("Overall Status of Companies in PTV" n.d.). A particularly successful sub-sector of IT has been the gaming industry: seven of the ten largest video game companies in Korea—Nexon, NCSOFT, Neowiz, and Hangame, to name a few—have formed the largest cluster in the country, even larger than the sector's presence in Seoul. Pangyo also serves as a strategic location for the semi-conductor industry, as it is close to both their management offices in Gangnam and their factories in Suwon and Icheon. Fifty semiconductor businesses have located their research centers within a stone's throw of each other and the headquarters of the Korea Semiconductor Industry Association (KSIA) in Pangyo Techno-Valley. Pangyo's bio-tech cluster is also alive and well, with large R&D centers—Institute Pasteur Korea, CHA Medical Center, Medipost, Sartorius, and the 22 bio-tech firms of the Korea BioPark consortium—and world-class medical centers such as Seoul National University Hospital, Samsung Medical Center, and Hyundai Asan Medical Center located nearby.

One notable aspect of Pangyo Techno Valley is its somewhat laid back, youthful work culture. Many residents observe that the relatively young workforce, the large presence of software engineers and tech workers, and numerous start-ups have created an environment where employees are quite relaxed, social, and informal—few people wear formal business attire, for example, in contrast to the crowds of suits seen in downtown Seoul. An energetic restaurant and café scene has also emerged to serve these workers. In addition, after the largest department store in Korea, the Hyundai, moved to Pangyo Techno Valley in 2015, Pangyo began to attract visitors from all over Seoul.

So far, it appears that Pangyo is not only becoming an economically vibrant new industrial city, but also fulfilling Gyeounggi province's goal of becoming a generator of national R&D output: in 1999 the province hosted fewer than 5% of the nation's R&D organizations, but with the addition of PTV, by 2014 the province had over 30% (Lee, Noh, and Seul 2017). That said, while about 91% of the companies in PTV are SMEs and fewer than 3% are conglomerates, the combined sales of the nine top conglomerates (such as SK Chemicals, SK telesys, POSCO ICT, and Samsung Techwin) still made up more than half of the total sales of the district (Lee Hyun-Jeong 2016). Plans to extend Pangyo into Techno-Valley 2 and 3 include designs to nurture some fourteen hundred additional start-ups by offering working spaces and consulting services at subsidized prices.

Strengths and Challenges Ahead

The main strength of the Pangyo Techno Valley project is its location: greenfield land within a 45-minute drive or 15-minute subway ride of downtown Seoul—a city housing half the South Korean population and the fourth largest metropolitan economy in the world—was very well placed to experience high demand. The main contribution of the local government was to guide this development pressure firmly through specific industrial policies and use industry expertise to uphold high standards for incoming resident firms.

Looking ahead, however, the small size of the district is likely to constrain the growth of the cluster; while PTV 2 and 3 will provide some room for expansion (subject to the same conditions and government intentions as PTV 1), the lack of developable real estate near the cluster is posing a challenge for novice companies. Soaring office rental fees over the past few years have made properties in Pangyo almost equivalent to those in Gangnam, pressuring some firms to reverse their decision to move out of the big city.[18] Pangyo was also designed to be an "eco-friendly" new city with the lowest targeted population density among all new city projects in Korea; there are large green spaces, numerous public parks, and an artificial waterway that runs through the town and connects it to green spaces in other cities in the district. One effect of this design, however, is that only 30,000 residential units are spread out over a land area of 9,400,000 m^2, including in several neighborhoods that feature only single-family detached housing.[19] The undersupply of housing in the area has forced employees of Pangyo's businesses to commute from Seoul or more affordable residential towns; this poses a particularly large problem considering the fact that most of the workforce is young but can't afford to start a family in the city where they work. In effect, Pangyo Techno Valley has become a successful new industry cluster, but the larger Pangyo New Town around it is not equipped to support its continued growth.

In our two cases in India and South Korea, we can observe important efforts invested in industry planning and development, which is a critical building block for creating vibrant cities. Without economic activity, those projects are doomed to failure. The planning aspect of industry development includes land planning, industry

---

18. Author interview with senior manager at Dasan and Handisoft (corporate tenants in Pangyo Techno-Valley 1), Jan. 11, 2018.
19. Author interview with senior manager in the Pangyo Cluster Team, Gyeounggi-do Business and Science Accelerator, Jan. 7, 2019.

positioning, supporting incentives, dedicated organization to promote investment, action plans divided into phases and measurable objectives. At the execution level, an aggressive promotional effort is important to bring early wins in the project and determine strategic partners to directly benefit from their experience and resources. Both Atal Nagar, India and Pangyo, South Korea have undertaken smart city or IT initiatives. Even though the success of those initiatives is not easily quantifiable, they provide some indications of how local authorities envision their city in the future and how technology can contribute to the success of those projects. New technologies will play a growing role in building vibrant cities in the future, and they should be integrated in the early stage planning of new city projects.

References

Bahga, Sarbjit. 2017. "Naya Raipur – India's 4th Planned Capital City Is Developing In Full Swing." World Architecture Community. July 5, 2017. https://worldarchitecture.org/articles/cvegh/naya_raipur__india_s_4th_planned_capital_city_is_developing_in_full_swing.html.

"C'garh Govt Signs Four MoU with Private Players." 2017. Https://Www.Outlookindia.Com/. July 11, 2017. https://www.outlookindia.com/newsscroll/cgarh-govt-signs-four-mou-with-private-players/1096506.

Chatterjee, Sudeshna, and Madhup Mazumder. 2008. "Shaping the Urban Landscape: Naya Raipur, the New Capital of Chhattisgarh." *Landscape Design* No. 21: 77–84.

"CSIDC Official Website." n.d. Accessed February 23, 2020. https://csidc.in/home2/index.php/en/.

Department of Industrial Policy and Promotion. n.d. "Ease of Doing Business in India 2016." http://industries.cg.gov.in/ease_of_doing_business.aspx.

"Electronic Manufacturing Cluster, Naya Raipur." n.d. https://csidc.in/emcprofile.pdf.

"EMC: IT & ITeS." n.d. Accessed February 24, 2020. http://emc.csidc.in/user/it-and-ites.php.

"EMC Official Website." n.d. Accessed February 23, 2020. https://emc.csidc.in/.

ET Bureau. 2015. "PM Narendra Modi Launches Smart Cities Mission, Says Centre Committed to Urban India." The Economic Times. June 26, 2015. https://economictimes.indiatimes.com/news/economy/policy/pm-narendra-modi-launches-smart-cities-mission-says-centre-committed-to-urban-india/articleshow/47811630.cms.

Government of India. 2015. "Prime Minister Launches Smart Cities, AMRUT, Urban Housing Missions." June 25, 2015. https://pib.gov.in/newsite/PrintRelease.aspx?relid=122788.

Government of India. n.d. "The Smart City Challenge Stage 2 – Smart City Proposal." http://smartcities.gov.in/upload/uploadfiles/files/Smart-City-Proposal_Naya%20Raipur.pdf.

Gyeounggi Provincial Government. n.d. "Pangyo Techno-Valley 1: Tenancy application guidebook." Public Data. Accessed November 9, 2019. https://www.pangyotechnovalley.org/html/community/dataroom.asp.

Hee Seok Choi. 2016. "Pangyo Techno Valley Posts over 70 Trillion Won in Sales in 2015." Korea Herald. May 24, 2016. http://www.koreaherald.com/view.php?ud=20160524000765.

Lee Hyun-Jeong. 2016. "Techno Valley - Korea's Start-up Hub." Korea Herald. July 15, 2016. http://www.koreaherald.com/view.php?ud=20160715000455.

Lee, Sam Youl, Meansun Noh, and Ji Yung Seul. 2017. "Government-Led Regional Innovation: A Case of 'Pangyo'IT Cluster of South Korea." *European Planning Studies* 25 (5): 848–866.

Maganti, Rahul. 2019. "Amaravati's Growing Pains: Soaring Land Prices, Falling Farm Fortunes." The Wire. January 31, 2019. https://thewire.in/urban/amaravati-soaring-land-prices-falling-farm-fortunes.

Mallick, Subhrojit. 2017. "Mahesh Lingareddy in Conversation: How Smartron Is Gearing up to Become a Global Force in Technology | Digit." December 7, 2017. https://www.digit.in/features/general/mahesh-lingareddy-in-conversation-how-smartron-is-gearing-up-to-become-a-global-force-in-technology-38538.html.

Myers, Joe. 2018. "India Is Building a Brand New City from Scratch." World Economic Forum. December 20, 2018. https://www.weforum.org/agenda/2018/12/india-is-building-a-city-from-scratch-to-attract-foreign-investors/.

Naya Raipur Development Authority. 2012. "Social Impact Assessment (SIA) & Resettlement Action Plan (RAP) for BRT Corridor in Naya Raipur Chhattisgarh." http://documents.worldbank.org/curated/pt/490631468041941701/pdf/RP819v60INDIA000290201300B0x377293B.pdf.

Naya Raipur Development Authority. n.d. "Naya Raipur Development Plan – 2031." https://navaraipuratalnagar.com/NRDARevampTheme/upload/23.pdf.

"Naya Raipur Development Plan – 2031." n.d. https://cghb.gov.in/NRDA_Guideline.pdf.

"Overall Status of Companies in PTV." n.d. Pangyo Techno Valley Website. Accessed November 9, 2019. https://www.pangyotechnovalley.org/eng/html/companies/consortium.asp.

Pangyo Techno Valley website. n.d. "Introduction." Accessed November 9, 2019b. http://www.pangyotechnovalley.org.

Pangyo Techno Valley website. n.d. Accessed November 9, 2019a. http://www.pangyotechnovalley.org.

Population Division - United Nations. 2018. "2018 Revision of World Urbanization Prospects." 2018. https://population.un.org/wup/.

Puri, Hardeep S. 2019. "How India Is Building Cities of the Future." The Economic Times. June 27, 2019. https://economictimes.indiatimes.com/news/economy/infrastructure/how-india-is-building-cities-of-the-future/articleshow/69964522.cms?from=mdr.

"Schneider Electric to Make India's First Integrated Green Field Smart City Project in Naya Raipur a Reality." n.d. Accessed February 24, 2020. https://www.se.com/in/en/about-us/press/press-release/2017/schneider-electric-to-make-india-first-integrated.

"Smart Cities Council India | News." n.d. Accessed February 24, 2020. https://india.smartcitiescouncil.com/category-news.

"Smart Cities of India- Mission 2022." 2018. IIFL. February 1, 2018. https://www.iifl.com/blogs/smart-cities-india-mission-2022.

"Smartron, Chhattisgarh Govt. Sign MoU to Incorporate Smart Technologies in State." 2017. July 10, 2017. https://www.outlookindia.com/newsscroll/smartron-chhattisgarh-govt-sign-mou-to-incorporate-smart-technologies-in-state/1096379.

"Statistics of Tenant Companies." n.d. Pangyo Techno Valley website. Accessed November 9, 2019. https://www.pangyotechnovalley.org/eng/html/companies/company_statistic.asp.

Traffic Infra Tech Magazine. 2013. "Naya Raipur: An Intersection of Transit, Urban Development and Urban Design - TrafficInfraTech Magazine." April 1, 2013. https://www.trafficinfratech.com/naya-raipuran-intersection-of-transit-urban-development-and-urban-design/.